56 Simply Illustrated Sermons

I0150344

by:
Dr. Christopher Bowen

Copyright © 2006 by Pastor Chris Bowen
All rights reserved
No portion of this work may be reproduced,
stored in a retrieval system, or transmitted in any
form or by any means electronic, mechanical
photocopy, recording, or any other except for
brief quotations in printed reviews, without the
prior permission of the Publisher.

Printing by: Lulu Press

USA ISBN 978-0-6151-6608-7

1

A CAKE WITH A PURPOSE

Props:
Butter, sugar, eggs, flour, salt, milk, big mixing
bowl, baking pans, finished cake

The ingredients of a cake are, butter, sugar, eggs, flour, salt, milk and vanilla. All these things in and of themselves don't taste good except the milk and sugar.

We can relate our life to the ingredients of a cake:

- Butter = divorce, betrayal of a friend
- Sugar = a promotion on your job, or when you graduated from college
- Eggs = molestation, rape
- Flour = losing your house, bad health
- Salt = death of a loved one
- Milk = meeting your true love

God has a way of taking things that are bad and making them good.

Romans 8:28 (KJV) And we know that all things work together for good to them that love God, to them who are the called according to his purpose.

All things may not be good but when we put it all together, it makes a pretty good tasting batter.

Don't you like to lick the spoon when someone is making a cake? Although it taste so good, too much of it will make you sick. So God has to mold you into the shape he wants you in.

Bring out the baking pans

God knew how he wanted you shaped before he made you.

Romans 8:29 (KJV) For whom he did foreknow, he also did predestinate to be conformed to the image of his Son, that he might be the firstborn among many brethren.

God takes the batter that taste so good and places it in a pan that is lightly greased, the anointing. With your anointed self you still aren't ready.

1. You are still wrestling with the fact of whether you are going to come to church or not.

2. You are still dealing whether or not you are going to forgive your brother or sister.

3. You are still wrestling with Salvation 101

So just as much as you want to be used, he wants to use you, so he preheats the oven and sets the timer.

He places the pan in the oven and allows it to bake. No matter how much you holler, Lord I am ready, He is looking at the timer and says "NO, a few more minutes."

Also, in baking you have to make sure that there is little to no traffic. Too much traffic makes the cake FALL. Be careful of how is walking in and out of your life. Relationships and soul ties. You have to be careful who you allow to speak into your life.

Then comes "TEST", are you ready yet? You can place a toothpick in the center of the cake, and if there is no cake on the toothpick, the cake is done. The problem with us is there is too much of us on the toothpick. So God allows us to cook a little longer.

Once we are done God will then give us a fresh anointing and lavish us with Frosting. You don't even have to ask anyone to come and get some of the cake. Once they see it, it's like, "oooo…Who's cake is this? I want some."

You don't have to show out, your gift will make room for you…And now we know our purpose and we can be used.

Then we can say like Paul in I Corinthians 4:17 – For this cause have I sent unto you Timotheus, who is my beloved son, and faithful in the Lord, who shall bring you into remembrance of my ways which be in Christ, as I teach every where in every church.

So what Paul is saying is that the abuse, the death of a loved one, your divorce, loosing your health, or house, is light. Then he says it is for a moment, all those years you cried, all the years you did with out.

It worketh, ETH, continually, even as you go through now it working a far more exceeding weight of glory...

I'd like to propose that whatever God is going to do is going to be so heavy that your problem will seem light.

2

> # ANGER is only one letter away from [D]ANGER!!

James 1:19-20 (NIV) My dear brothers, take note of this: _Everyone should be quick to listen, slow to speak and slow to become angry_, [20] for man's anger does not bring about the righteous life that God desires.

Ephesians 4:26-27 (NIV) "_In your anger do not sin_" : Do not let the sun go down while you are still angry, [27] and do not give the devil a foothold. (BECAUSE IF YOU DO...YOU GIVE THE DEVIL A FOOTHOLD...)

➢ Tonight I want to deal with a subject that has the effect of touching many of us.
➢ ANGER
➢ Anger is listed in the Bible nearly 300 times.
➢ How do you deal with anger?
➢ Anger can be dealt with in many areas and forms.
➢ How does your anger come out?

Exodus 32:15-19 (NIV) Moses turned and went down the mountain with the two tablets of the Testimony in his hands. They were

inscribed on both sides, front and back. [16] The tablets were the work of God; the writing was the writing of God, engraved on the tablets. [17] When Joshua heard the noise of the people shouting, he said to Moses, "There is the sound of war in the camp." [18] Moses replied: "It is not the sound of victory, it is not the sound of defeat; it is the sound of singing that I hear." [19] *When Moses approached the camp and saw the calf and the dancing, his anger burned and he threw the tablets out of his hands, breaking them to pieces at the foot of the mountain.*

> Even though we feel that Moses had a right to be angry…
> God did not allow his excuse…
> We make excuses for our behavior… such as
> Well, she made me mad
> God doesn't intend on my being a door mat
> Or even SIN MAKES ME MAD…
> But God didn't honor Moses for his anger.
> Look what happens in Exodus 34:1

Exodus 34:1 (NIV) The LORD said to Moses, "*Chisel out two stone tablets like the first ones*, and I will write on them the words that were on the first tablets, which you broke.

Exodus 34:4 (NIV) *So Moses chiseled out two stone tablets like the first ones* and went up Mount Sinai early in the morning, as the LORD had commanded him; and he carried the two stone tablets in his hands. [5] Then the LORD came down in the cloud and stood there with him and proclaimed his name, the LORD. [6] And he passed in front of Moses,

proclaiming, "The LORD, the LORD, the compassionate and gracious God, _slow to anger_, abounding in love and faithfulness, [7] maintaining love to thousands, and forgiving wickedness, rebellion and sin....

➤ God himself chiseled out the first set of tablets out of the rock...
➤ But the second set Moses had to cut out...
➤ Since he sinned through his anger...
➤ He had to pay a price.

The Bible teaches us that we are to be more like HIM...

➤ Slow to anger...
➤ Do you have a problem getting ANGRY quickly...
➤ HOT tempered???
➤ HOT headed???
➤ Then we are not being like CHRIST!!!

John 18:10-11 (NIV) Then _Simon Peter,_ [11] Jesus commanded Peter, " _who had a sword, drew it and struck the high priest's servant, cutting off his right ear._ Put your sword away! Shall I not drink the cup the Father has given me?"

Luke 22:50-51 (NIV) And one of them _struck the servant of the high priest, cutting off his right ear._ [51] But Jesus answered, "_No more of this!_" And he touched the man's ear and healed him.

1 Timothy 2:8 (NIV) I want men everywhere to lift up holy hands in prayer, *without anger or disputing.*

James 1:19-20 (NIV) My dear brothers, take note of this: *Everyone should be quick to listen, slow to speak and slow to become angry,* [20] for man's anger does not bring about the righteous life that God desires.

> ➢ Our anger can lead us to danger is we are not careful…
> ➢ Anger will destroy us
> ➢ Eat us like a cancer…
> ➢ And then laugh at us…
> ➢ Making us feel guilty…
> ➢ Embarrassed… and even
> ➢ UNSAVED….

ANGER IS ONLY ONE LETTER AWAY FROM DANGER… WE REALLY DON'T WANT OT CROSS THE LINE…BECAUSE THE NEXT STEP ISN'T VERY PRETTY!!!

Psalms 55:22 (NIV) Cast your cares on the LORD and he will sustain you; he will never let the righteous fall.

3

Are your Bags too heavy?

Props: You will need SEVERAL suitcases and a Large upright set of scales, in a couple of suitcases (closest to you) have helium balloons with them that say Stress, Anxiety, Jealousy, Unforgiveness, Hatred, Bitterness, Gossip, Sin. Each balloon needs a string on it...like a kite...with one of the above words written on both sides of the paper, so when they come out of the suitcase...the congregation can read them.

Have on the platform in a trash bag, regular balloons without helium, but blown up...with the same words on them.

The object will be...that you will fill the empty suitcase with them...then at the end of the message...you will open the other suitcase and they will fly out...

Hebrews 12:1-2 (KJV) Wherefore seeing we also are compassed about with so great a cloud of witnesses, let us lay aside every weight, and the sin which doth so easily beset us, and let us run with patience the

race that is set before us, [2] Looking unto Jesus the author and finisher of our faith; who for the joy that was set before him endured the cross, despising the shame, and is set down at the right hand of the throne of God.

As Kathy and I prepared for our trip to Europe, I consistently told her… not to pack to heavy. I knew that we would be traveling nearly 6000 miles, and I didn't want to pack a bunch of stuff that we didn't need AND…………………………………………

> ➤ There is a 50 per bag weight limit at the airport.
> ➤ On our departure…
> ➤ She assured me that she only took what we absolutely had to have
> ➤ 2 LARGE bags…
> ➤ As we weighed them in…
> ➤ They came to a total of 99 pounds…
> ➤ Only one pound away from being… TOO much according to the airport…
> ➤ SHE CUT IT CLOSE…

TODAY… I WANT TO ASK YOU….ARE YOUR BAGS TOO HEAVY?

WHAT KIND OF BAGGAGE ARE YOU TRAVELING WITH…

ARE YOU OVERLOADED….

Colossians 3:5-9 (KJV)   Mortify therefore your members which are upon the earth;

fornication, uncleanness, inordinate affection, evil concupiscence, and covetousness, which is idolatry: [6] For which things' sake the wrath of God cometh on the children of disobedience: [7] In the which ye also walked some time, when ye lived in them. [8] But now ye also put off all these; anger, wrath, malice, blasphemy, filthy communication out of your mouth. [9] Lie not one to another, seeing that ye have put off the old man with his deeds; [10] And have put on the new man, which is renewed in knowledge after the image of him that created him:

Colossians 3:12 (KJV) Put on therefore, as the elect of God, holy and beloved, bowels of mercies, kindness, humbleness of mind, meekness, longsuffering;

➢ When we boarded our connecting flight from Paris to Rome…
➢ The flight attended asked if we were traveling with luggage…
➢ We told him yes… he asked for the receipt…
➢ We showed him…and he punched in some numbers and told us to board…
➢ RIGHT THEN I thought…we are traveling 6000 miles with TOO MUCH BAGGAGE
➢ When we arrived in Rome… You guessed it…
➢ NO LUGGAGE…
➢ Everyone pulled theirs off the belt… to leave us alone at an empty carrousel
➢ They assured us…that if we could make it one day…. They would have our bags to us…

- But one day came and went…
- 6000 miles… and not even a tooth brush
- The next day came..
- And the next…
- After traveling more than 12,000, we realized that we could survive on much less baggage then we though.
- We left with 2 large , 99 pound bags…
- Toured Rome, Venice, Pisa, Siena, Florence, Paris, and even Houston…
- And came home…with a small carry on bag…
- BUT we made it…

The cars in Europe are MUCH smaller.

- If we had ALL of our luggage
- And all the luggage with those with us…
- Plus the 4 of us that went…
- We would have NEVER made it to the airport..
- Why…because we had too much baggage.

Many Christians miss the flight…because they are carrying TOO MUCH BAGGAGE…

- Many Christians will miss the flight to heaven… because they are weighed down with too much baggage.
- You are traveling with hatred, bitterness (Put in suit case here)
- It is weighing you down…
- Destroying your health

- ➤ Tiring you out…

You need to unload some things on God and
Lighten up…your load.
Some things don't matter.

MOSES
- ➤ He was carrying to much baggage…
- ➤ He told God…not to use him because he
  stuttered in his speech
- ➤ He told God…that he couldn't be
  used…because…he had baggage… he killed a
  man…now he was a murder…
- ➤ He became angry and smote the
  rock…because of his baggage…
- ➤ He broke the commandments upon the
  ground…because of his baggage…
- ➤ AND his baggage…eventually made him miss
  the promised land….
- ➤ ARE YOU GOING TO LET YOUR
  BAGGAGE ….KEEP YOU OUT OF
  YOUR PROMISED LAND?

- ➤ They thought I would stress about the
  luggage…
- ➤ But I didn't… because…it really didn't
  matter…
- ➤ It was a little inconvenient… but … we had
  fun shopping everyday for something new to
  wear…
- ➤ We had to wash our sox out by hand and dry
  them on a blow dryer…

➢ But… it really didn't matter and it most definitely didn't ruin the trip.

1 Peter 2:1-3 (KJV) Wherefore laying aside all malice, and all guile, and hypocrisies, and envies, and all evil speakings, ² As newborn babes, desire the sincere milk of the word, that ye may grow thereby: ³ If so be ye have tasted that the Lord is gracious. (taste and see that the Lord is GOOD!)

4

Bootleg Saints

Props:
You need a couple of Legs, and a coupled boots....BOOTLEG... You also need several things that are bootleg. You need to have a copy of a movie... that looks real...but then someone gets up and walks out in the movie and you can tell it was boot leg...something like 'White Chics' that you can show the clip
A Bible; A Bottle; A DVD;
A poorly done cover of a Bootleg DVD; A gospel CD; A bootleg CD

1 Corinthians 10:1-5 (NIV) For I do not want you to be ignorant of the fact, brothers, that our forefathers were all under the cloud and that they all passed through the sea. [2] They were all baptized into Moses in the cloud and in the sea. [3] _They all ate the same spiritual food [4] and drank the same spiritual drink; for they drank from the spiritual rock_ that accompanied them, and that rock was Christ. [5] Nevertheless, God was not pleased with most of them; their bodies were scattered over the desert.

1 Corinthians 10:6-13 (NIV) Now these things occurred as examples to keep us from

19

setting our hearts on evil things as they did. [7] Do not be idolaters, as some of them were; as it is written: "The people sat down to eat and drink and got up to indulge in pagan revelry." [8] *We should not commit sexual immorality*, as some of them did--and in one day twenty-three thousand of them died. [9] *We should not test the Lord*, as some of them did--and were killed by snakes. [10] And *do not grumble*, as some of them did--and were killed by the destroying angel. [11] These things happened to them as examples and were written down as warnings for us, on whom the fulfillment of the ages has come. [12] So, *IF you think you are standing firm, be careful that you don't fall*! [13] No temptation has seized you except what is common to man. And *God is faithful*; he will not let you be tempted beyond what you can bear. But when you are tempted, *he will also provide a way out so that you can stand up under it*.

In essence…what the scripture is saying is…

- ➤ Don't be foolish enough to think…that because your daddy is a preacher and your momma is a saint…that you have the right to heaven because of them
- ➤ Don't be foolish enough to think…because you can sit at the table with the distinguished that you own the company…
- ➤ Don't be foolish enough to think…You can live any old life style and still make it to heaven…
- ➤ Even though…they were all baptized into Moses…they are didn't make it

- Even though…they all ate and drank the same thing…they didn't get the same reward…
- YOU GOTTA LIVE IT…
- YOU GOTTA HAVE IT…
- YOU GOTTA SHOW IT…
- YOU GOTTA SPEAK IT…
- YOU GOTTA PROCLAIM IT…

- Some of you boot leg movies
- Some of you boot leg liquor
- Some of you have boot leg "GOSPEL" CDS you are listening to and praising God with
- And Some of us are just Bootleg Saints

WHAT IS A BOOTLEG SAINT?

- Bootleg… is something done… illegal
- A bootleg Saint is one who is trying to act like something he or she is not
- Carrying the Bible on Sunday and the Bottle on Sunday
- Dancing in the spirit on Sunday and in the "spirits" on Saturday
- Speaking in Tongues as you leave… and in a cursing tongue by the time you get home.

Matthew 23:23-28 (NIV) "Woe to you, teachers of the law and Pharisees, you hypocrites! You give a tenth of your spices-- mint, dill and cummin. But you have neglected the more important matters of the law--justice, mercy and faithfulness. _You should have practiced the latter, without neglecting the former._ [24] You blind guides!

You strain out a gnat but swallow a camel. [25] "Woe to you, teachers of the law and Pharisees, you hypocrites! *You clean the outside of the cup and dish, but inside they are full of greed and self-indulgence.* [26] Blind Pharisee! *First clean the inside of the cup and dish, and then the outside also will be clean.* [27] "Woe to you, teachers of the law and Pharisees, you hypocrites! *You are like whitewashed tombs, which look beautiful on the outside but on the inside are full of dead men's bones and everything unclean.* [28] In the same way, *on the outside you appear to people as righteous but on the inside you are full of hypocrisy and wickedness.*

You might be a bootleg Christian if:

➤ You use someone else's church bulletin to get a discount at the restaurant
➤ You hold credentials just to get a discount at the bookstore
➤ You have more than one set of credentials to park free at hospitals
➤ You use your Popular Mechanics Ministerial card to get into jail to see your friends
➤ You want store credit in the candy store in the church
➤ You get mad if your birthday isn't in the directory even if you haven't been here in two years.
➤ You can't attend another Sunday School class because your teacher is out sick
➤ You don't even go to Sunday School
➤ You pay your tithes in Monopoly Money

➤ You lie about your age, to get a senior discount or a closer parking spot at the church.
➤ You get mad when pastor cant remember your name…when you haven't been here in 4 years.
➤ You bring in your Big Mac or chips to 'watch the show' this morning

Galatians 5:16-23 (NIV) So I say, _live by the Spirit_, and you will not gratify the desires of the sinful nature. [17] For _the sinful nature desires what is contrary to the Spirit_, and the Spirit what is contrary to the sinful nature. They are in conflict with each other, so that you do not do what you want. [18] But if you are led by the Spirit, you are not under law. [19] _The acts of the sinful nature are obvious: sexual immorality, impurity and debauchery;_ [20] _idolatry and witchcraft; hatred, discord, jealousy, fits of rage, selfish ambition, dissensions, factions_ [21] _and envy; drunkenness, orgies, and the like._ I warn you, as I did before, that those who live like this will not inherit the kingdom of God. [22] But _the fruit of the Spirit is love, joy, peace, patience, kindness, goodness, faithfulness,_ [23] _gentleness and self-control._ Against such things there is no law.

Judges 12:5-6 (NIV) The Gileadites captured the fords of the Jordan leading to Ephraim, and whenever a survivor of Ephraim said, "Let me cross over," the men of Gilead asked him, "Are you an Ephraimite?" If he replied, "No," [6] they said, "All right, say 'Shibboleth.'" If he said, "Sibboleth," because he could not

pronounce the word correctly, they seized him and killed him at the fords of the Jordan. Forty-two thousand Ephraimites were killed at that time.

5

BURN BABY BURN

Props:
You will need a huge blaze of fire with me on the platform. Give everyone a match…but it can NOT be real. Maybe the wooden ones, you can cut the head off and use a red marker to make it look real. Have a small tag attacked… KEEP THE FLAME BURNING!

Leviticus 6:8-13 (NIV) The LORD said to Moses: [9] "Give Aaron and his sons this command: 'These are the regulations for the burnt offering: The burnt offering is to remain on the altar hearth throughout the night, till morning, and *the fire must be kept burning on the altar.* [10] The priest shall then put on his linen clothes, with linen undergarments next to his body, and *shall remove the ashes* of the burnt offering that the fire has consumed on the altar and place them beside the altar. [11] Then *he is to take off these clothes and put on others,* and carry the ashes outside the camp to a place that is ceremonially clean. [12] *The fire on the altar must be kept burning; it must not go out.* Every morning the priest is to *add firewood* and arrange the burnt offering on the fire and burn the fat of the fellowship offerings on it.

13 The *fire must be kept burning on the altar continuously; it must not go out.*

WE HAVE GOT TO KEEP THE FIRE BURNING ON THE ALTAR

- ➢ We must keep things hot for God
- ➢ The world is offering so many things to our young people
- ➢ If they can not find something new and exciting in the church, they will find it in the world.
- ➢ We must keep the devil on the move
- ➢ We must keep our mind made up…that we are going to serve and praise Him.

The bible says that the priest would remove the ashes from the day before….Ashes represent yesterdays blessings

Philippians 3:13-14 (NIV) Brothers, I do not consider myself yet to have taken hold of it. But one thing I do: *Forgetting what is behind and straining toward what is ahead,* 14 I press on toward the goal to win the prize for which God has called me heavenward in Christ Jesus.

Isaiah 43:18-19 (NIV) "*Forget the former things; do not dwell on the past.* 19 See, I am doing a new thing!

- ➢ God is into change
- ➢ God is into new things
- ➢ How many of you all like new things?

26

- ➤ Nothing wrong with wearing a suit from the thrift store
- ➤ BUT it sure is nice to wear the new off of something every now and then.
- ➤ The message never changes
- ➤ But the approach or method does

WE WILL ACCEPT CHANGES:
1. In our life
2. In our life styles
3. In our hair color
4. In our clothing size.
5. In our financial standings
6. In our way of life
7. BUT... WE DON'T WANT TO REACH OUT TO ANYONE UNLESS IT IS THE WAY WE HAVE ALWAYS DONE IT.

The priest would change clothes...

Isaiah 61:3 (NIV) .....put on a garment of praise instead of a spirit of despair. They will be called oaks of righteousness, a planting of the LORD for the display of his splendor.

- ➤ The priest realized...it was time for a change.
- ➤ The priest realized...he had to make preparation from one challenge to the next.

Take off the spirit of heaviness ... put on garments of praise

- ➤ God has not become cold, the saints have

27

- ➢ God has not become lazy, the saints have
- ➢ God has not become weak, the saints have
- ➢ God has not become stagnant, the saints have
- ➢ God is still God…the Altar is still hot

How can we keep our altar hot… when we only go to it once a week, or even 5 times a week.

- ➢ The priest had to go clean it out every day
- ➢ The priest had to go add wood to it every day
- ➢ We must do the same thing in our spiritual life

IS YOUR ALTAR BLAZING FOR CHRIST?

ARE YOU STILL AT THE PLACE THAT WHEN YOU HIT YOUR ALTAR…THAT GOD STILL HAS A HOT WORD FOR YOU?

Hebrews 13:8 (NIV) Jesus Christ is the same yesterday and today and forever.

6

CALL IT OUT!!!

What do you need from the LORD?

Today we are going to call it out…

> **Philippians 4:6 (NIV)   Do not be anxious about anything, but in everything, by prayer and petition, with thanksgiving, _present your requests to God._**

> **Romans 4:17 tells us that we have the power to _CALL THINGS OUT THAT BE NOT…AS THOUGH THEY WERE!!!!_**

PROPS:
You will need to have as many instruments on the platform with you as possible. Each instrument should have a spot on a chair…as if it is an orchestra. You will also need a mega-phone, and for each person a small index card that says…TODAY I HAVE CALLED IT OUT…(They will fill this out and turn it in) Also, see prop idea at the end of this chapter.

> **Ezekiel 37:1-10 (NIV)   The hand of the LORD was upon me, and he brought me out by the Spirit of the LORD and set me in the middle**

of a valley; it was full of bones. [2] He led me back and forth among them, and I saw a great many bones on the floor of the valley, bones that were very dry. [3] He asked me, "Son of man, can these bones live?" I said, "O Sovereign LORD, you alone know." [4] Then he said to me, "*Prophesy to these bones* and say to them, 'Dry bones, *hear the word of the LORD!* [5] This is what the Sovereign LORD says to these bones: *I will make breath enter you, and you will come to life. [6] I will attach tendons to you and make flesh come upon you and cover you with skin; I will put breath in you, and you will come to life.* Then you will know that I am the LORD."' [7] So I prophesied as I was commanded. And as I was prophesying, *there was a noise, a rattling sound, and the bones came together,* bone to bone. [8] I looked, and *tendons and flesh appeared on them and skin covered them*, but there was no breath in them. [9] Then he said to me, "Prophesy to the breath; prophesy, son of man, and say to it, 'This is what the Sovereign LORD says: Come from the four winds, O breath, and breathe into these slain, that they may live.'" [10] So *I prophesied as he commanded me, and breath entered them; they came to life and stood up on their feet*--a vast army.

➢ Ezekiel prophecied to the bones...
➢ He took power and authority
➢ He called out life and not death
➢ He took authority over death
➢ He spoke life back into existence

WHAT ARE YOU CALLING OUT???

- Victory or Defeat
- Life or Death
- Health or Pain
- Poverty or Plenty
- Love or Hate

Philippians 4:8 (NIV)   Finally, brothers, whatever is true, *whatever is noble, whatever is right, whatever is pure, whatever is lovely, whatever is admirable--if anything is excellent or praiseworthy--<u>think about such things.</u>*

- Take a moment and get mad at the devil
- Take a moment and count your blessings!!!

Habakkuk 2:2-3 (NIV)   Then the LORD replied: *"<u>Write down the revelation and make it plain</u>....* [3] ...Though it linger, wait for it; it will certainly come and will not delay.

- Now... on the card that you have been given this morning... call it out
- Write down what you want...
- Those in the balcony...throw them over the rail
- Those on the floor... pick those up and bring your with them ....
- To the altar.

1 King 18:21-29 (NIV)   Elijah went before the people and said, "How long will you waver between two opinions? If the LORD is God, follow him; but if Baal is God, follow him." But the people said nothing. [22] Then Elijah

said to them, *"I am the only one of the Lord's prophets left, but Baal has four hundred and fifty prophets.* ²³ Get two bulls for us. Let them choose one for themselves, and let them cut it into pieces and put it on the wood but not set fire to it. I will prepare the other bull and put it on the wood but not set fire to it. ²⁴ Then you *call on the name of your god,* and *I will call on the name of the LORD. The god who answers by fire--he is God."* Then all the people said, "What you say is good." ²⁵ Elijah said to the prophets of Baal, "Choose one of the bulls and prepare it first, since there are so many of you. Call on the name of your god, but do not light the fire." ²⁶ So they took the bull given them and prepared it. Then they called on the name of Baal from morning till noon. *"O Baal, answer us!" they shouted. But there was no response; no one answered.* And they danced around the altar they had made. ²⁷ At noon Elijah began to taunt them. "Shout *louder!" he said. "Surely he is a god! Perhaps he is deep in thought, or busy, or traveling. Maybe he is sleeping* and must be awakened." ²⁸ So they shouted louder and slashed themselves with swords and spears, as was their custom, until their blood flowed. ²⁹ Midday passed, and they continued their frantic prophesying until the time for the evening sacrifice. But there was no response, no one answered, no one paid attention.

Prop:
You will need something clear that you can add water too...and some type of wood that will burn even when wet.

---

1 Kings 18:33-39 (NIV) Elijah arranged the wood at the altar, cut the bull into pieces and laid it on the wood. Then he said to them, "Fill four large jars with water and pour it on the offering and on the wood." ³⁴ "Do it again," he said, and they did it again. "Do it a third time," he ordered, and they did it the third time. *³⁵ The water ran down around the altar and even filled the trench. ³⁶ At the time of sacrifice, the prophet Elijah stepped forward and prayed: "O LORD, God of Abraham, Isaac and Israel, let it be known today that you are God in Israel and that I am your servant and have done all these things at your command. ³⁷ Answer me, O LORD, answer me, <u>so these people will know that you, O LORD, are God</u>, and that you are turning their hearts back again." ³⁸ Then the fire of the LORD fell and burned up the sacrifice, the wood, the stones and the soil, and also licked up the water in the trench. ³⁹ When all the people saw this, they fell prostrate and cried, <u>"The LORD--he is God! The LORD--he is God!"</u>*

- ➤ Elijah called God out... to prove that he was God...
- ➤ Elijah knew when he prayed...that God was going to show up
- ➤ Elijah did this that God may be glorified and that...
- ➤ People would turn back to God

WHAT ARE YOU CALLING OUT?????

7

Casting Stones

PROPS:
YOU WILL NEED THE STAIR CASE
PACKED WITH STONES...BIG ONES...
AND REGULAR SIZED ONES...LOTS AND
LOTS OF THEM. ALSO...WE WILL NEED
TO PASS OUT TO EACH PERSON A LARGE
STONE...ABOUT THE SIZE OF TENNIS
BALLS...

John 8:1-11 (NIV) But Jesus went to the Mount of Olives. [2] At dawn he appeared again in the temple courts, where all the people gathered around him, and he sat down to teach them. [3] The teachers of the law and the Pharisees brought in a *woman caught in adultery.* They made her stand before the group [4] and said to Jesus, "Teacher, *this woman was caught in the act of adultery.* [5] In the Law Moses commanded us to stone such women. Now what do you say?" [6] They were using this question as a trap, in order to have a basis for accusing him. But Jesus bent down and started to write on the ground with his finger. [7] When they kept on questioning him, he straightened up and said to them, *"If any one of you is without sin, let him be the first to* *throw a stone at her." [8] Again he stooped down and wrote on the ground. [9] At this, those who heard began to go away one at a time, the older ones first, until only Jesus was left, with the woman still standing there. [10] Jesus straightened up and asked her, "Woman, where are they? Has no one condemned you?" [11] "No one, sir," she said. "Then neither do I condemn you," Jesus declared. "Go now and leave your life of sin."*

It always has stuck in my mind that Peter denied Christ

We know that Peter came back and more than 3000 were saved (Acts 2:41) at one time…but we still cast stones at him…because he denied Christ 3 times.

Matthew 26:33-35 (NIV) Peter replied, *"Even if all fall away on account of you, I never will."* [34] "I tell you the truth," Jesus answered, *"this very night, before the rooster crows, you will disown me three times."* [35] But Peter declared, *"Even if I have to die with you, I will never disown you." And all the other disciples said the same.*

But we overlook what Christ was saying just 2 scriptures before this:

AFTER TAKING COMMUNION TOGETHER:

Matthew 26:30-32 (NIV) When they had sung a hymn, they went out to the Mount of Olives. [31] Then Jesus told them, *"This very night you*

will __all__ fall away on account of me, for it is written: "'I will strike the shepherd, and the sheep of the flock will be scattered.'

Matthew 26:36-46 (NIV)   Then Jesus went with his disciples to a place called Gethsemane, and he said to them, "Sit here while I go over there and pray." [37] He took Peter and the two sons of Zebedee along with him, and he began to be sorrowful and troubled. [38] Then he said to them, "My soul is overwhelmed with sorrow to the point of death. Stay here and keep watch with me." [39] Going a little farther, he fell with his face to the ground and prayed, "My Father, if it is possible, may this cup be taken from me. Yet not as I will, but as you will." [40] *Then he returned to his disciples and found them sleeping.* "Could you men not keep watch with me for one hour?" he asked Peter. [41] "Watch and pray so that you will not fall into temptation. The spirit is willing, but the body is weak." [42] *He went away __a second time__ and prayed,* "My Father, if it is not possible for this cup to be taken away unless I drink it, may your will be done." [43] *When he came back, he again found them sleeping,* because their eyes were heavy. [44] *So he left them and went away once more and prayed the __third time,__ saying the same thing.* [45] *Then he returned to the disciples and said to them, "__Are you still sleeping and resting?__* Look, the hour is near, and the Son of Man is betrayed into the hands of sinners. [46] Rise, let us go! Here comes my betrayer!"

- After Jesus is arrested… we find in verse 56 of Matthew 26… *"**Then all the disciples deserted him and fled.**"*
- Why is it that we only remember Peter doing it
- Why don't we realize that the other all did the same thing
- Why can we see someone else's fault… but not our own ****

Matthew 7:3-5 (NIV) *"Why do you look at the* **speck of sawdust** *in your brother's eye and pay no attention to the* **plank in your own eye?** [4] *How can you say to your brother, 'Let me take the speck out of your eye,' when all the time there is a plank in your own eye?* [5] *You hypocrite, first* **take the plank out of your own eye, and then you will see clearly to remove the speck from your brother's eye.**

Ways that we forsake him:

- When we put down… or allow others to put down our brother/sister
- When we have an open opportunity to testify…but don't
- When we have the right to walk away from dirty talk and jokes…but laugh anyway.
- When we…knowing in our heart… sin and act like it is ok.
- When He wakes you up in the night to talk to you…and you roll over and go back to sleep.
- When you step over your Bible to get to your newspaper
- When you over eat and under fast

Mark 8:34-38 (NIV) Then he called the crowd to him along with his disciples and said: "If anyone would come after me, he must *deny himself* and *take up his cross* and *follow me.* [35] For whoever wants to save his life will lose it, but whoever loses his life for me and for the gospel will save it. [36] What good is it for a man to gain the whole world, yet forfeit his soul? [37] Or what can a man give in exchange for his soul? [38] *If anyone is ashamed of me and my words* in this adulterous and sinful generation, *the Son of Man will be ashamed of him* when he comes in his Father's glory with the holy angels."

8

TIMEX...TAKE A LICKING...AND KEEP ON TICKING....

PROPS:
You need to **LARGE CLOCKS...ALL OVER THE PLATFORM!** You need on huge... at least 3 foot clock...on the wall... with **TIMEX** on it... You also need some clips of Coyote and Road Runner...see below. **YOU NEED A CD** of a clock ticking...played throughout the entire message.

How many of you remember Coyote and Road Runner? No matter how many times...Road Runner out did Coyote...He still kept on ticking. Coyote would get right back up and start again...knowing that he was going to get blown up by dynamite, have a bolter fall on his head, or the bridge to collapse, just as he got on it to cross over to the other side... COYOTE.... TOOK A LICKING AND KEPT ON TICKING!!!

- As children of God... We get one little bump on the head from Satan...and we are ready to give up!!!
- We must stand our ground....
- Take our Authority...
- And let the enemy know...
- WE GONNA KEEP ON TICKING!!!

2 Samuel 18:19-31 (NIV) **Now Ahimaaz son of Zadok said, "Let me run and take the news to the king that the LORD has delivered him from the hand of his enemies." [20] "You are not the one to take the news today," Joab told him. "You may take the news another time, but you must not do so today, because the king's son is dead." [21] Then Joab said to a Cushite, "Go, tell the king what you have seen." The Cushite bowed down before Joab and ran off. [22] Ahimaaz son of Zadok again said to Joab, _"Come what may, please let me run_ behind the Cushite." But Joab replied, "My son, why do you want to go? You don't have any news that will bring you a reward." [23] He said, _"Come what may, I want to run."_ So Joab said, "Run!" Then Ahimaaz ran by way of the plain and outran the Cushite.**

- Ahimaaz was excited...he wanted to share his excitement with someone...
- He just wanted to run...
- He knew that there was news to share...
- He wanted to be the messenger
- So when he couldn't be the messenger...
- He just asked if he could run...
- And finally the King gave in and told him to RUN...

2 Samuel 18:24-31 (NIV) While David was sitting between the inner and outer gates, the watchman went up to the roof of the gateway by the wall. As he looked out, he saw a man running alone. [25] The watchman called out to the king and reported it. The king said, "If he is alone, he must have good news." And the man came closer and closer. [26] Then the watchman saw another man running, and he called down to the gatekeeper, "Look, another man running alone!" The king said, "He must be bringing good news, too." [27] The watchman said, "It seems to me that the first one runs like Ahimaaz son of Zadok." "He's a good man," the king said. "He comes with good news." [28] Then Ahimaaz called out to the king, "All is well!" He bowed down before the king with his face to the ground and said, "Praise be to the LORD your God! He has delivered up the men who lifted their hands against my lord the king." [29] The king asked, "Is the young man Absalom safe?" Ahimaaz answered, "I saw great confusion just as Joab was about to send the king's servant and me, your servant, but *I don't know what it was."* [30] The king said, "Stand aside and wait here." So he stepped aside and stood there. 31 Then the Cushite arrived and said, "My lord the king, hear the good news! The LORD has delivered you today from all who rose up against you."

➢ Then he Out ran the messenger…
➢ LOOK AT THIS … KING DAVID…SAID…DO YOU HAVE GOOD NEWS….
➢ Ahimaaz…says YES… ALL IS WELL…

- THEN in verse 29 we find out that King asked him about what he saw…and he said…
- I saw some confusion…but I don't know what it was…
- HE WAS TICKING…
- He didn't get caught up with the mess….
- He had the Message of Deliverance…
- He proclaimed… The LORD HAS DELIVERED YOU TODAY FROM ALL OF THOSE WHO ROSE AGAINST YOU!!!
- He was TICKING….YOU HEAR ME… HE WAS TICKING…

How about:

- Paul and Silas… They took at beating…was put into prison… but they kept on singing…they took a licking…but kept on ticking…
- You know the story… God… brought them out…and the jailer got saved.
- Remember Job…The lost it all… his children, his flock, his stock, his money and his health…
- Yet he told his wife when she told him to curse God and die…. "You speak like a crazy women…
- HE TOOK A LICKING BUT KEPT ON TICKING.
- Joseph… was betrayed by his brothers and pronounced dead to his father… yet he was sold into foreign land and became the Kings

right hand man... and had to feed his starving family that betrayed him...

- HE TOOK A LICKING AND KEPT ON TICKING.
- Daniel...was cast into the lions den...left for dead... supper for his furry friends... yet he did not give up... he made pillows out of their fur and blankets out of their paws... and slept until morning...
- HE TOOK A LICKING AND KEPT ON TICKING
- David at the young age of a teenager...faced the battle of Goliath... a nine foot tall giant... the giant laughed at him and knew that he could crush him with one pounce... yet...David said... You come to me with a spear and a sword...yet I come to you in the name of the Lord... and as you know...he killed the giant....

- HE TOOK A LICKING BUT KEPT ON TICKING...

You need to realize today... that God may let you go through something... but it is not to destroy you... it is to make your tick louder...

- REMEMBER...WHAT THE DEVIL MEANT FOR BAD... GOD CAN TURN IT AROUND AND MAKE IT GOOD.... .AND GOOD ENOUGH TO BLESS YOU!!

TICK OUT LOUD..........REAL LOUD!!!

45

- ➤ Many saints today are afraid to tick to loud… afraid the devil may hear them…
- ➤ But we need to be ticking so loud that he knows he better get out of our way…
- ➤ Because we are coming through…taking everything that belongs to us…

WE NEED TO BE MORE LIKE AHIMAAZ…

- ➤ We need to be excited to run with good news…
- ➤ NOT THE BAD…
- ➤ We must keep on going… regardless of how the circumstances look around us…
- ➤ We have to keep be like TIMEX…
- ➤ WE MUST TAKE OUR LICKING…BUT KEEP ON TICKING!!!!

9

Dancing with God!

PROPS:
You will need some slow dance music and some fast dance music

2 Samuel 6:12-16 (NIV) Now King David was told, "The LORD has blessed the household of Obed-Edom and everything he has, because of the ark of God." So David went down and brought up the ark of God from the house of Obed-Edom to the City of David with rejoicing. [13] When those who were carrying the ark of the LORD had taken six steps, he sacrificed a bull and a fattened calf. [14] *David, wearing a linen ephod*, danced before the LORD with all his might, [15] while he and the entire house of Israel brought up the ark of the LORD with shouts and the sound of trumpets. [16] As the ark of the LORD was entering the City of David, Michal daughter of Saul watched from a window. And when she saw King David leaping and dancing before the LORD, she despised him in her heart.

➢ David brings the ark to Jerusalem
➢ Thus, he transforms the city into a worship center and it becomes the capital of Israel

- David danced alone…
- A linen Ephod in vs 14…is the lightest weight of clothing
- He was prepared to worship
- He took off all his heavy garments before his journey
- We too must prepare for our blessing
- We too must be prepared to worship and dance
- How many of you wore something uncomfortable tonight.
- How about those shoes… are they easy to kick off and so you can dance?

THE HIGHEST EXPRESSION OF JOY IS A "DANCE"

When you think on the word "GUIDANCE" you will see the word "DANCE" at the end. I remember reading that doing God's will is a lot like dancing. When two people try to lead, nothing feels right. The movement does not flow with the music, and everything is quite uncomfortable and jerky. When one person realizes that, and lets the other lead, both bodies begin to flow with the music. One gives gentle cues, perhaps with a nudge to the back or by pressing lightly in one direction or another. It's as if two become one body, moving beautifully. The dance takes surrender, willingness, and attentiveness from one person and gentle guidance and skill from the other. My eye draws back to the word, "GUIDANCE".

When I saw "G" I thought of God, followed by "U" and "I". "God, "U" and "I" dance." God you and I dance! I realized that I had to become willing to trust that I would get guidance about my life. But, I must be willing to let God lead.

> **2 Samuel 6:20-22 (NIV) When David returned home to bless his household, Michal daughter of Saul came out to meet him and said, "How the king of Israel has distinguished himself today, disrobing in the sight of the slave girls of his servants as any vulgar fellow would!" [21] David said to Michal, *"It was before the LORD, who chose me rather than your father or anyone from his house* when he appointed me ruler over the Lord's people Israel--I will celebrate before the LORD. [22] *I will become even more undignified than this,* and I will be humiliated in my own eyes. But by these slave girls you spoke of, I will be held in honor."**

➤ Disrobing means to lay aside his royal garments

➤ Appearing only in his tunic…which is what the slaves were wearing.

➤ Remember…Michal daddy … Saul… is the one that was trying to kill him…

➤ David determined in his heart… it didn't matter that she didn't like it

➤ It didn't matter that her daddy didn't like it

➤ It was not an offering to them … but to GOD.

Not everyone will dance with you!!!

Sometimes you gotta dance all by yourself!!!

Here are some things that God won't ask you on Judgment day:

- ➢ God won't ask what kind of car you drove...but how many you drove to church
- ➢ God won't ask how big your house is... but how many you invited into your house
- ➢ God won't ask about he clothes in your closet...but how many you helped to clothe
- ➢ God won't ask how much salary you made...but he will ask if you compromised your character to get it
- ➢ God won't ask for your job title, but he will ask if you preformed your job to the best of your ability
- ➢ God won't ask how many friends you had... but he will ask to how many people were you friendly
- ➢ God won't ask what neighborhood you lived in... but he will ask how you treated your neighbors
- ➢ God won't ask the color of your skin... but he will ask about the content of your character

Ecclesiastes 3:4 (NIV) (there is a time for everything), a time to mourn and a time to dance,

Jeremiah 31:1-4 (NIV) "At that time," declares the LORD, "I will be the God of all the clans

of Israel, and they will be my people." ² This is what the LORD says: "The people who survive the sword will find favor in the desert; I will come to give rest to Israel." ³ The LORD appeared to us in the past, saying: *"I have loved you with an everlasting love; I have drawn you with loving-kindness.* ⁴ *I will build you up again and you will be rebuilt,* O Virgin Israel. Again *you will take up your tambourines and go out to <u>dance with the joyful.</u>*

10

Dismembered Members

Props:
You will need a full manikin standing with all the body parts. As you talk about the body going through the different phases, you can rip off a part of the body.

We as a body are suppose to be whole. No one part is better than the other...

Romans 12:1-5 (NIV) Therefore, I urge you, brothers, in view of God's mercy, to *offer your bodies as living sacrifices*, holy and pleasing to God--this is your spiritual act of worship. [2] Do not conform any longer to the pattern of this world, but be transformed by the *renewing of your mind*. Then you will be able to test and approve what God's will is-- his good, pleasing and perfect will. [3] For by the grace given me I say to every one of you: Do not think of yourself more highly than you ought, but rather think of yourself with sober judgment, in accordance with the measure of faith God has given you. [4] Just as each of us has one body with many members, and these members do not all have the same function, [5] so in Christ *we*

who are many form one body, and each member belongs to all the others.

Quote: Cut off your nose to spite your face…

The Bible says:

1 Corinthians 12:12-26 (NIV) _The body is a unit,_ though it is made up of many parts; and though all its parts are many, they form one body. So it is with Christ. [13] For we were all baptized by one Spirit into _one body_-- whether Jews or Greeks, slave or free--and we were all given the one Spirit to drink. [14] Now the _body is not made up of one part but of many._ [15] If the foot should say, "Because I am not a hand, I do not belong to the body," it would not for that reason cease to be part of the body. [16] And if the ear should say, "Because I am not an eye, I do not belong to the body," it would not for that reason cease to be part of the body. [17] If the whole body were an eye, where would the sense of hearing be? If the whole body were an ear, where would the sense of smell be? [18] But in fact God has arranged the parts in the body, every one of them, just as he wanted them to be. [19] If they were all one part, where would the body be? [20] As it is, _there are many parts, but one body._ [21] _The eye cannot say to the hand, "I don't need you!"_ And the head cannot say to the feet, "I don't need you!" [22] On the contrary, those parts of the body _that seem to be weaker are indispensable,_ [23] and the parts that we think are less honorable we treat with special honor. And the parts that are unpresentable are treated with special modesty, [24] while our presentable parts need

no special treatment. But God has combined the members of the body and has given greater honor to the parts that lacked it, ²⁵ so that there should be no division in the body, but that its parts should have equal concern for each other. ²⁶ _If one part suffers, every part suffers with it; if one part is honored, every part rejoices with it._

The reason we are falling short…is because we are not lining up with the Word of God!!!

➢ We are going around deformed.
➢ Jealousy - Hand
➢ Addictions- Arm
➢ Pride - Hand
➢ Gossip - Arm

1 Corinthians 12:27-31 (NIV) Now you _are the body of Christ,_ and each one of you is a part of it. ²⁸ And in the church God has appointed first of all apostles, second prophets, third teachers, then workers of miracles, also those having gifts of healing, those able to help others, those with gifts of administration, and those speaking in different kinds of tongues. ²⁹ Are all apostles? Are all prophets? Are all teachers? Do all work miracles? ³⁰ Do all have gifts of healing? Do all speak in tongues? Do all interpret? ³¹ But eagerly desire the greater gifts. And now I will show you the most excellent way.

➢ Wanting someone else's talents… (TEAR OFF THE LEG)

- ➢ Put the arm where the leg goes
- ➢ The leg where the arm goes…etc…
- ➢ Doesn't this seem silly….
- ➢ But this is how we look when we get out of Gods will.

Galatians 6:3-5 NIV If anyone thinks he is something when he is nothing, he deceives himself. [4] Each one should test his own actions. Then he can take pride in himself, without comparing himself to somebody else, [5] for each one should carry his own load.

- ➢ We need each other
- ➢ No man is an island by himself
- ➢ We fall, slip and stumble
- ➢ We need someone to help pick us up.

11

'Cirrhosis of the Giver'

PROP:
You need a glass container again with a **BIG
BOX** of "corn flakes.
You will fill the container- the small one, then
press down and pour more in, press down,
shake together and running over.

Cirrhosis of the liver- Is a disease when the liver
hardens because of excessive formation of
connecting tissue followed by contractions.

Cirrhosis of the giver- Is a disease when the giver
hardens because of excessive greediness connected
to the hip follow by contraction when given.

There is a disease which is particularly harsh in this
part of the twentieth century. It is called cirrhosis of
the giver. It was actually discovered about 34 AD
and ran a terminal course in a couple named
Annanias and Sapphira (Acts 5). It is an acute
condition which renders the patient's hand
immobile, when it attempts to move from the
billfold to the offering plate. The remedy is to
remove the afflicted from the house of God, since it
is clinically observable that this condition disappears

in alternate environments such as golf courses, or clubs, or restaurants.

Acts 5:1-11 (NIV) Now a man named Ananias, together with his wife Sapphira, also sold a piece of property. [2] With his wife's full knowledge he _kept back part of the money for himself,_ but brought the rest and put it at the apostles' feet. [3] Then Peter said, "Ananias, how is it that Satan has so filled your heart that _you have lied to the Holy Spirit_ and have kept for yourself some of the money you received for the land? [4] Didn't it belong to you before it was sold? And after it was sold, wasn't the money at your disposal? _What made you think of doing such a thing? You have_ not _lied_ to men but _to God."_ [5] When Ananias heard this, he fell down and died. And great fear seized all who heard what had happened. [6] Then the young men came forward, wrapped up his body, and carried him out and buried him. [7] _About three hours later his wife came in,_ not knowing what had happened. [8] Peter asked her, "Tell me, is this the price you and Ananias got for the land?" _"Yes," she said, "that is the price."_ [9] Peter said to her, "How could you agree to test the Spirit of the Lord? Look! The feet of the men who buried your husband are at the door, and they will carry you out also." [10] At that moment _she fell down at his feet and died._ Then the young men came in and, finding her dead, carried her out and buried her beside her husband. [11] _Great fear seized the whole church_ and all who heard about these events.

There is a story about a man who died and went to Heaven. There, he made this comment concerning his use of money on earth. He said, "***What I spent, I lost; what I saved, I left; and what I gave, I have.***" We do not lose what we give. We send it on before us that there may be treasure in Heaven.

Matthew 6:19-21 (NIV) "Do not store up for yourselves treasures on earth, where moth and rust destroy, and where thieves break in and steal. [20] *But store up for yourselves treasures in heaven, where moth and rust do not destroy, and where thieves do not break in and steal.* [21] *For where your treasure is, there your heart will be also.*

Matthew 22:15-21 (NIV) Then the Pharisees went out and laid plans to trap Jesus in his words. [16] They sent their disciples to him along with the Herodians. "Teacher," they said, "we know you are a man of integrity and that you teach the way of God in accordance with the truth. You aren't swayed by men, because you pay no attention to who they are. [17] Tell us then, what is your opinion? *Is it right to pay taxes to Caesar or not?"* [18] But Jesus, knowing their evil intent, said, "You hypocrites, why are you trying to trap me? [19] Show me the coin used for paying the tax." They brought him a denarius, [20] and he asked them, "Whose portrait is this? And whose inscription?" [21] "Caesar's," they replied. Then he said to them, *"Give to Caesar what is Caesar's, and to God what is God's."*

- We don't like to pay taxes…but we like driving on good roads and high ways.
- We don't like paying taxes…but we like for our children to be in good schools…
- We don't like to pay taxes…but we like to draw a check at retirement…even if it is not enough…

Malachi 3:8-12 (NIV) "Will a man rob God? Yet you rob me. "But you ask, 'How do we rob you?' "In tithes and offerings. [9] _You are under a curse_--the whole nation of you--because you are robbing me. [10] Bring the whole tithe into the storehouse, that there may be food in my house. _Test me in this_," says the LORD Almighty, "and _see if I will not throw open the floodgates of heaven and pour out so much blessing that you will not have room enough for it._ [11] I will _prevent pests from devouring your crops, and the vines in your fields will not cast their fruit_," says the LORD Almighty. [12] "Then all the nations will call you blessed, for yours will be a delightful land," says the LORD Almighty.

- We don't like to give…but we like having Gods promises
- We don't like to give…yet we want Gods healing
- We don't like to give …but we want the abundant blessing
- We don't like to give…but want all our needs to be met

Luke 6:37-38 (NIV) "Do not judge, and you will not be judged. Do not condemn, and you will not be condemned. Forgive, and you will be forgiven. [38] _Give, and it will be given to you. A good measure, pressed down, shaken together and running over, will be poured into your lap._ For with the measure you use, it will be measured to you."

12

DO YOU HAVE VISION OR DIVISION IN YOUR VISION

Today, I want to take a look at two similar words, yet they are SO distinctively different.

Those two words would be: VISION and DIVISION...

Webster's describes Vision as - A SUPERNATURAL APPEARANCE THAT CONVEYS A REVELATION; (or) AN OBJECT OF IMAGINATION

Webster's also describes Di-Vision –as - THE STATE OF BEING DIVIDED...

Di= Dead

So di-vision= Dead Vision

Thank God for all the good help that God has brought to the "Tabernacle but there can only be ONE vision" Two visions is called DI-Vision...more than one.

Anything with 2 heads...is considered a MONSTER.

That is why we have:
- ➤ One Sunday School Superintendent and her Assistant
- ➤ One Choir director
- ➤ One Teacher of each class...with assistants
- ➤ One Day Care Director
- ➤ One President and CEO of a company
- ➤ One Spouse... ☺
- ➤ Can you imagine the chaos with 2????

Lets take a look at Di-vision first:

Isaiah 59:1-4 (NIV) Surely the arm of the LORD is not too short to save, nor his ear too dull to hear. [2] But your iniquities _have separated you from your God;_ your sins have hidden his face from you, so that he will not hear. [3] For your hands are stained with blood, your fingers with guilt. Your lips have spoken lies, and your tongue mutters wicked things. [4] No one calls for justice; no one pleads his case with integrity. They rely on empty arguments and speak lies; they conceive trouble and give birth to evil.

- ➤ The rest of this chapter goes on to tell us what happens where there is division.

Mark 3:25-26 (NIV) If a house is _divided against itself, that house cannot stand._ [26] And _if Satan opposes himself and is divided, he cannot stand;_ his end has come.

UNITED WE STAND…BUT DIVIDED…WE FALL…NO MAN IS AN ISLAND…

1 Corinthians 12:21-27 (NIV) The eye cannot say to the hand, "I don't need you!" And the head cannot say to the feet, "I don't need you!" [22] On the contrary, those parts of the body that seem to be weaker are indispensable, [23] and the parts that we think are less honorable we treat with special honor. And the parts that are unpresentable are treated with special modesty, [24] while our presentable parts need no special treatment. But God has combined the members of the body and has given greater honor to the parts that lacked it, [25] so that _there should be no division in the body,_ but that its parts should have equal concern for each other. [26] If one part suffers, every part suffers with it; if one part is honored, every part rejoices with it. [27] Now you are the body of Christ, and each one of you is a part of it.

James 1:5-8 (NIV) If any of you lacks wisdom, he should ask God, who gives generously to all without finding fault, and it will be given to him. [6] But when he asks, _he must believe and not doubt,_ because he who doubts is like a wave of the sea, blown and tossed by the wind. [7] That man should not think he will receive anything from the Lord; [8] _he is a double-minded man, unstable in all he does._

NOW LETS LOOK AT VISION:

PAUL HAD A VISION

Acts 18:7-11 (NIV) **Then Paul left the synagogue and went next door to the house of Titius Justus, a worshiper of God.** **8 Crispus, the synagogue ruler, and his entire household believed in the Lord; and many of the Corinthians who heard him believed and were baptized. 9 One night the Lord spoke to Paul _in a vision_: "Do not be afraid; keep on speaking, do not be silent. 10 For I am with you, and no one is going to attack and harm you, because I have many people in this city." 11 So Paul stayed for a year and a half, teaching them the word of God.**

In this next passage of scripture… we find:
  ➢ A priest named Zachariah
  ➢ He was married to Elizabeth
  ➢ They were both upright, the Bible Says, before God.
  ➢ While they were worshipping…look what happened

Luke 1:11-25 (NIV) **Then an angel of the Lord appeared to him, standing at the right side of the altar of incense. 12 When Zechariah saw him, he was startled and was gripped with fear. 13 But the angel said to him: _"Do not be afraid, Zechariah; your prayer has been heard. Your wife Elizabeth will bear you a son, and you are to give him the name John._ 14 He will be a joy and delight to you, and many will rejoice because of his birth, 15 for he will be great in the sight of the Lord. He is never to take wine or other fermented drink, and _he will be filled with the Holy Spirit even from birth._ 16 Many of the people of Israel will**

he bring back to the Lord their God. [17] And he will go on before the Lord, in the spirit and power of Elijah, to turn the hearts of the fathers to their children and the disobedient to the wisdom of the righteous--to make ready a people prepared for the Lord." [18] Zechariah asked the angel, "How can I be sure of this? I am an old man and my wife is well along in years." [19] The angel answered, *"I am Gabriel. I stand in the presence of God, and I have been sent to speak to you and to tell you this good news.* [20] *And now you will be silent and not able to speak until the day this happens, because you did not believe my words, which will come true at their proper time."* [21] Meanwhile, the people were waiting for Zechariah and wondering why he stayed so long in the temple. [22] When he came out, he could not speak to them. *They realized he had seen a vision in the temple,* for he kept making signs to them but remained unable to speak. [23] When his time of service was completed, he returned home. [24] *After this his wife Elizabeth became pregnant* and for five months remained in seclusion. [25] "The Lord has done this for me," she said. "In these days he has shown his favor and taken away my disgrace among the people."

WHEN THERE IS VISION...THERE SHOULD BE MANIFESTATION!!

Luke 1:57-64 (NIV)   When it was time for Elizabeth to have her baby, she gave birth to a son. [58] Her neighbors and relatives heard that the Lord had shown her great mercy, and they shared her joy. [59] On the eighth day they came to circumcise the child, and they were going to name him after his father Zechariah, [60] but his mother spoke up and said, "No! He is to be called John." [61] They said to her, "There is no one among your relatives who has that name." [62] Then they made signs to his father, to find out what he would like to name the child. [63] He asked for a writing tablet, and to everyone's astonishment he wrote, "His name is John." [64] *Immediately his mouth was opened and his tongue was loosed, and he began to speak, praising God.*

Acts 9:10-17 (NIV) In Damascus there was a disciple named Ananias. *The Lord called to him in a vision, "Ananias!"* "Yes, Lord," he answered. [11] The Lord told him, "Go to the house of Judas on Straight Street and ask for a man from Tarsus named Saul, for he is praying. [12] In a vision he has seen a man named Ananias come and place his hands on him to restore his sight." [13] "Lord," Ananias answered, "I have heard many reports about this man and all the harm he has done to your saints in Jerusalem. [14] And he has come here with authority from the chief priests to arrest all who call on your name." [15] But the Lord said to Ananias, "Go! This man is my chosen instrument to carry my name before the Gentiles and their kings and before the people of Israel. [16] I will show him how much he must suffer for my name." [17] *Then Ananias went to the house and entered it. Placing his hands on Saul, he said, "Brother Saul, the Lord--Jesus, who appeared to you on the road as you were coming here--has sent me so that you may see again and be filled with the Holy Spirit."*

Habakkuk 2:2-3 (NIV)... the LORD replied: *"Write down the revelation* (VISION) *and make it plain on tablets so that a herald may run with it.* [3] For the revelation (VISION) awaits an appointed time; it speaks of the end and will not prove false. Though it linger, wait for it; it will certainly come and will not delay.

13

Does the shoe fit?

Props:
You will need 5 different kinds of shoes:
Sneakers; Running; Flip Flops; Combat Boots;
and Baby shoes. You will also need as many
other pairs of shoes on the platform that you can
get...LOTS of shoe boxes... you can use the
song "These boots are made for walking.

The Bible has much to say about shoes.

How the shoe resembles our lives: (hold up a dress shoe)

> Every shoe has a maker
> Every shoe is made for a purpose
> Every shoe has a tongue, eyes, and a sole
> For repairs it has to go to the right person
> The hide was provided by a sacrifice

Ruth 4:7-10 (NIV) Now in earlier times in Israel, for the redemption and transfer of property to become final, one party _took off his sandal (shoe)_ and gave it to the other.

This was the method of legalizing transactions in Israel. [8] So the kinsman-redeemer said to Boaz, "Buy it yourself." And he *removed his sandal.* (shoe) [9] Then Boaz announced to the elders and all the people, "Today you are witnesses that I have bought from Naomi all the property of Elimelech, Kilion and Mahlon. [10] *I have also acquired Ruth the Moabitess, Mahlon's widow, as my wife,* in order to maintain the name of the dead with his property, so that his name will not disappear from among his family or from the town records. Today you are witnesses!"

➢ Boaz takes off his shoe as a binding contract to buy land from Elimelech.
➢ By taking off his shoe as a testimony this also confirmed that he was redeeming his bride.
➢ That shoe was a testimony to all Israel that Boaz was redeeming Ruth to be his Bride. So, as I read this custom of the Jews, and the testimony of this shoe, I began to think how shoes represent the Christians of today.
➢ See if you can recognize any???

1. THE SNEAKERS

➢ The SNEAKERS think they can sneak by with their sin like David did with Bathsheba.
➢ Ananias and Sapphira tried to sneak money out of the kitty to hoard it up for themselves. Acts 5

> Achan hid the money and garments in his tent thinking that no one else would find it. Joshua 7

John 10:1 (NIV) "I tell you the truth, the man who does not enter the sheep pen by the gate, but climbs in by some other way, is a thief and a robber.

> Some people think that they can sneak in on Momma's skirt tail
> Other feel that if they join the church ...they can sneak in
> Even others think that if they are baptized many times...they can sneak their way into heaven.

2. THE RUNNING SHOES

Some Christians are RUNNING from GOD like Jonah.

Some Christians are RUNNING to GOD like Zacchaeus.

Some Christians are RUNNING for GOD like Paul. Thank GOD for these saints!!!

3. THE BABY SHOES

In every church there are some Christians wearing baby shoes.

The Apostle Paul said in 1 Corinthians 3:1 (NIV)
Brothers, I could not address you as spiritual but as
worldly--mere infants in Christ.

- ➤ A baby always cries for attention
- ➤ Never wants to change even when dirty
- ➤ And always wants the milk.

**Hebrews 5:12-14 (NIV) In fact, though by this
time you ought to be teachers, you need
someone to teach you the elementary truths
of God's word all over again. You need milk,
not solid food! [13] Anyone who lives on milk,
being still an infant, is not acquainted with
the teaching about righteousness. [14] But
solid food is for the mature, who by constant
use have trained themselves to distinguish
good from evil.**

4. THE FLIP FLOPS

- ➤ This group makes promises that they never keep.
- ➤ They say they will show up…but never do.
- ➤ They are for you one day…and not the next
- ➤ God sent them this week…next week he sent them across town…
- ➤ Just like Peter told CHRIST, "You can depend on me" yet he denied Christ three time before the cock crowed.
- ➤ Before their night was over, he "did a flip-flop."

**Matthew 21:28-31 (NIV) "What do you think?
There was a man who had two sons. He went**

to the first and said, 'Son, go and work today in the vineyard.' [29] "'I will not,' he answered, but *later he changed his mind and went.* [30] "Then the father went to the other son and said the same thing. He answered, *'I will, sir,' but he did not go.* [31] "Which of the two did what his father wanted?" "The first," they answered. Jesus said to them, "I tell you the truth, the tax collectors and the prostitutes are entering the kingdom of God ahead of you.

5. THE COMBAT BOOTS

- Christians should be wearing combat boots with steal toes…
- There is something wrong when you attend church and don't get your toes stepped on from time to time.
- It is those who are wearing flip flops…that get their feeling hurt.
- Those wearing combat boots…are strong and tough
- They are glad you are getting them out of their comfort zone…
- And on the meat of the word…
- They don't get offended…they become strong warriors.

I like these that know and understand we are in a battle.

GOD called us to raise the dead, heal the sick, and defeat the devil:

"Devil, these boots are made for walking and I'm gonna walk all over you."

Luke 9:62 (NIV) Jesus replied, "No one who puts his hand to the plow and looks back is fit for service in the kingdom of God."

WHAT KIND OF SHOES ARE YOU
WEARING????
    A. SNEAKERS
    B. RUNNING
    C. FLIP FLOP
    D. BABY SHOES
    E. COMBAT BOOTS

14

Dynamite comes in small packages

'A Sermon on WISDOM'

PROPS:
You need something looking like a stick of dynamite, on the screen. You need a video of a building being blown up. The Atlanta Stadium would be great. Also, you will need a giant: Ant; Locust ; Coney (Europe Rabbit); Lizard

Proverbs 3:13–18 (NIV) *Blessed is the man who finds wisdom,* the man who gains understanding, [14] for she is more profitable than silver and yields better returns than gold. [15] She is more precious than rubies; nothing you desire can compare with her. [16] Long life is in her right hand; in her left hand are riches and honor. [17] Her ways are pleasant ways, and all her paths are peace. [18] She is a tree of life to those who embrace her; those who lay hold of her will be blessed.

1 Kings 3:5-12 (NIV) At Gibeon the LORD appeared to Solomon during the night in a dream, and God said, *"Ask for whatever you want me to give you."* [6] Solomon answered, "You have shown great kindness to your servant, my father David, because he was faithful to you and righteous and upright in heart. You have continued this great kindness to him and have given him a son to sit on his throne this very day. [7] "Now, O LORD my God, you have made your servant king in place of my father David. But I am only a little child and do not know how to carry out my duties. [8] Your servant is here among the people you have chosen, a great people, too numerous to count or number. [9] *So give your servant a discerning heart to govern your people and to distinguish between right and wrong.* For who is able to govern this great people of yours?" [10] The Lord was pleased that Solomon had asked for this. [11] So God said to him, "Since you have asked for this and not for long life or wealth for yourself, nor have asked for the death of your enemies but for discernment in administering justice, [12] I will do what you have asked. *I will give you a wise and discerning heart,* so that there will never have been anyone like you, nor will there ever be.

In 1 Kings 3: 16-28, There is a story of 2 prostitutes that have babies and one rolls over on hers and it dies…..Solomon gives a wise ruling.

1 Kings 3:16-28 (NIV) Now two prostitutes came to the king and stood before him. [17] One of them said, "My lord, this woman and I

live in the same house. I had a baby while she was there with me. [18] The third day after my child was born, this woman also had a baby. We were alone; there was no one in the house but the two of us. [19] "During the night this woman's son died because she lay on him. [20] So she got up in the middle of the night and took my son from my side while I your servant was asleep. She put him by her breast and put her dead son by my breast. [21] The next morning, I got up to nurse my son-- and he was dead! But when I looked at him closely in the morning light, I saw that it wasn't the son I had borne." [22] The other woman said, "No! The living one is my son; the dead one is yours." But the first one insisted, "No! The dead one is yours; the living one is mine." And so they argued before the king. [23] The king said, "This one says, 'My son is alive and your son is dead,' while that one says, 'No! Your son is dead and mine is alive.'" [24] Then the king said, "Bring me a sword." So they brought a sword for the king. [25] He then gave an order: "Cut the living child in two and give half to one and half to the other." [26] The woman whose son was alive was filled with compassion for her son and said to the king, "Please, my lord, give her the living baby! Don't kill him!" But the other said, "Neither I nor you shall have him. Cut him in two!" [27] Then the king gave his ruling: "Give the living baby to the first woman. Do not kill him; she is his mother." [28] When all Israel heard the verdict the king had given, they held the king in awe, because they saw that he had wisdom from God to administer justice.

1 Kings 4:30-31 (NIV) *Solomon's wisdom was greater than the wisdom of all the men* of the East, and greater than all the wisdom of Egypt. *[31] He was wiser than any other man...*

- In verse 32, it says that Solomon wrote more than 3000 proverbs.

Proverbs 30:24-28 (NIV) "Four things on earth are small, yet they are extremely wise: [25] *Ants* are creatures of little strength, yet they store up their food in the summer; [26] *coneys* are creatures of little power, yet they make their home in the crags; [27] *locusts* have no king, yet they advance together in ranks; [28] a *lizard* can be caught with the hand, yet it is found in kings' palaces.

God uses the small things of this world to teach us wisdom. Often times we think that it is in big, glamorous, highly things... but God uses ants, coney's, locusts and lizards to teach us wisdom.

15

Follow the SON!!!

Props:
Have Sunflowers throughout the stage. Give everyone a small sunflower and to others a small packet of sunflower seeds, as a prop. You will also need Sunflower- Vegetable oil, Margarine made with Sunflower oil, Sunflower seeds, cereal with sunflower seeds in it…. Etc.

Each morning as the Sunflower opens…it opens in the direction that faces the sun. As the sun moves from the east and makes its way to the west to set for the evening, the sunflower never allows anything to get in its way to follow the sun…wherever it might go.

There are some lessons we could learn from the Sunflower:

1. **The Sunflower always follows the sun regardless of its path**

Romans 15:4-6 (NIV) For everything that was written in the past was written to teach us, so that through endurance and the encouragement of the Scriptures we might have hope. [5] May the God who gives

endurance and encouragement give you a spirit of unity among yourselves *as you follow Christ Jesus,* [6] so that with one heart and mouth you may glorify the God and Father of our Lord Jesus Christ.

➢ The sunflower always follows the sun each and every day of its existence/ WE MUST FOLLOW THE SON…EVERYDAY OF OUR LIFE.
➢ The sunflower understand that the sun is the source of its strength and its dependency to life/ WE MUST ALSO REALIZE THAT THE SON…IS OUR SOURCE OF STRENGTH AND POWER.

2. <u>The Sunflower must stand tall and often…by itself</u>

Romans 14:12 (NIV) So then, each of us will give an account of himself to God.

2 Corinthians 5:10 (NIV) For we must all appear before the judgment seat of Christ, that each one may receive what is due him for the things done while in the body, whether good or bad.

➢ The Sunflower stands from 6 to 10 feet tall / WE MUST STAND TALL FOR CHRIST
➢ The Sunflower springs into bloom, a full 12 inches in bloom./ WE MUST BLOOM FOR GOD… AND LET OUR GLORY SHINE FOR HIM

3. **The Sunflower is recognized worldwide for its beauty.**

Psalms 27:4 (NIV) One thing I ask of the LORD, this is what I seek: that I may dwell in the house of the LORD all the days of my life, _to gaze upon the beauty of the LORD_ and to seek him in his temple.

➤ David said… I want to gaze upon the BEAUTY of the Lord
➤ If God is beautiful and he is in us…. We are also beautiful
➤ WHEN WE LOOK AND ACT LIKE HIM…

4. **The Sunflower is a source of strength to others.**

Romans 15:1-2 (NIV) _We who are strong ought to bear with the failings of the weak_ and not to please ourselves. [2] Each of us should please his neighbor for his good, _to build him up._

➤ The Sunflower produces healthy Vegetable Oil
➤ Sunflower seeds---filled with protein as a snack
➤ Sunflower kernels are filled with important vitamins and minerals.
➤ The nutrients of a Sunflower is considered to be a powerhouse compared to no other for what it offers in health foods.

➤ WE MUST BE AN ENCOURAGER TO OUR BROTHERS AND SISTERS
➤ WE MUST LIFT THEM UP… BE A STEPPING STONE…NOT A STUMBLING BLOCK.

5. The Sunflower is a producer of seeds.

John 12:24-26 (NIV) I tell you the truth, unless a kernel of wheat falls to the ground and dies, it remains only a single seed. But if it dies, it produces many seeds. [25] The man who loves his life will lose it, while the man who hates his life in this world will keep it for eternal life. [26] Whoever serves me must follow me; and where I am, my servant also will be…

➤ One bloom on a sunflower has more than 1000 seeds
➤ That is a 1000% increase
➤ We are happy with 30, 60, 100…. But this 1 plant has the capability of growing 1000 more just like it
➤ How many people will you lead to the Lord in your life time.

Mark 4:8 (NIV) Still other seed fell on good soil. It came up, grew and produced a crop, multiplying thirty, sixty, or even a hundred times."

Deuteronomy 1:11 (NIV) May the LORD, the God of your fathers, increase you a thousand times and bless you as he has promised!

16

Get "CONNECTED"

PROPS:
Pass out to everyone a piece of chain that can be connected to each other, or several 6 inch length of 1 inch PVC and several connectors that can put the pipes together. Also have a large object on platform, such as two large PVC pipes with a connector. There needs to be three signs to tape on 4 kings 1) Joram – King of Israel 2) Jehoshaphat- King of Judah 3) Mesha- king of Moab…. 4) Elisha- man of God

---

Whatever you are connected to….you will become like it

When we partake of communion…the reason we do so, is because of the two words that make up the word communion…..Common Union

1 Corinthians 11:23-26 NIV For I received from the Lord what I also passed on to you: The Lord Jesus, on the night he was betrayed, took bread, [24] and when he had given thanks, he broke it and said, "This is my body, which is for you; do this in remembrance of me." [25] In the same way, after supper he took the cup, saying, "This

cup is the new covenant in my blood; do this, whenever you drink it, in remembrance of me." ²⁶ For whenever you eat this bread and drink this cup, you proclaim the Lord's death until he comes.

We are becoming like him…we are partaking and connecting to Him…therefore … we are becoming like him.

1 Corinthians 12:21-26 NIV The eye cannot say to the hand, "I don't need you!" And the head cannot say to the feet, "I don't need you!" ²² On the contrary, those parts of the body that seem to be weaker are indispensable, ²³ and the parts that we think are less honorable we treat with special honor. And the parts that are unpresentable are treated with special modesty, ²⁴ while our presentable parts need no special treatment. But _God has combined the members of the body_ and has given greater honor to the parts that lacked it, ²⁵ so that there should be no division in the body, but that its parts should have equal concern for each other. ²⁶ If one part suffers, every part suffers with it; if one part is honored, every part rejoices with it.

- As LFT gets bigger, I hear more and more… You loose the personal touch…
- You better get over that….
- You better get connected to something BIG
- The Bible says in Deut… 1 can put 1000 demons to running
- 2 can put 10,000 flying

➢ You better get connecting to something as BIG as you can.

YOU SEE....WHAT YOU ARE CONNECTED TO... BECOMES YOU

➢ Elisha...became a part of Elijah...where you saw one...you automatically saw the other.
➢ Where you saw Naomi....there was Ruth
➢ Where you find Joshua...not to far behind was Caleb
➢ Where you saw Paul....there was Silas....Not just in the good times...but through the bad times as well.

In 2 Kings 3, we find a story of "connection"

2 Kings 3:1-14 (NIV) Joram son of Ahab became king of Israel in Samaria in the eighteenth year of Jehoshaphat king of Judah, and he reigned twelve years. [2] He did evil in the eyes of the LORD, but not as his father and mother had done. He got rid of the sacred stone of Baal that his father had made. [3] Nevertheless he clung to the sins of Jeroboam son of Nebat, which he had caused Israel to commit; he did not turn away from them. [4] Now Mesha king of Moab raised sheep, and he had to supply the king of Israel with a hundred thousand lambs and with the wool of a hundred thousand rams. [5] But after Ahab died, the king of Moab rebelled against the king of Israel. [6] So at that time King Joram set out from Samaria and mobilized all Israel. [7] He also sent this message to Jehoshaphat king of Judah: "The king of Moab has rebelled against me. Will

you go with me to fight against Moab?" "I will go with you," he replied. "I am as you are, my people as your people, my horses as your horses." [8] "By what route shall we attack?" he asked. "Through the Desert of Edom," he answered. [9] So the king of Israel set out with the king of Judah and the king of Edom. After a roundabout march of seven days, the army had no more water for themselves or for the animals with them. [10] "What!" exclaimed the king of Israel. "Has the LORD called us three kings together only to hand us over to Moab?" [11] But Jehoshaphat asked, "Is there no prophet of the LORD here, that we may inquire of the LORD through him?" An officer of the king of Israel answered, "Elisha son of Shaphat is here. He used to pour water on the hands of Elijah." [12] Jehoshaphat said, "The word of the LORD is with him." So the king of Israel and Jehoshaphat and the king of Edom went down to him. [13] Elisha said to the king of Israel, "What do we have to do with each other? Go to the prophets of your father and the prophets of your mother." "No," the king of Israel answered, "because it was the LORD who called us three kings together to hand us over to Moab." [14] Elisha said, "As surely as the LORD Almighty lives, whom I serve, if I did not have respect for the presence of Jehoshaphat king of Judah, I would not look at you or even notice you.

We find that King Joram, King of Israel, Connected with King Jehoshaphat, king of Judah. They partnered up to go against King Mesha, the King of Moab to overtake him.

We find that as friends…they didn't always walk the highway…but they walked the desert. Vs 8

The two kings… ran out of supplies in verse 9 and cried out for help from a prophet of the Lord. They called up Elisha

In vs. 12 they recognized that the word of the Lord was with Him (Elisha) Elisha was connected to God.

John 1:1 NIV In the beginning was the Word, and the Word was with God, and the Word was God.

> ➤ Elisha had the word of God with him… so God was with him and he was with God.

In vs. 13 and 14 Elisha asks the King of Israel (Joram)… "What do we have in common?" Because Joram rebelled against God.

Elisha tells Joram… because you have connected yourself with the King of Judah (Jehoshaphat)… which means "Praise" then I will help…otherwise, he would not have given him the time of day.

> ➤ Joram was brought out because of who he was hanging with…Jehoshaphat.
> ➤ Look who you are hanging out with
> ➤ Look to your right and look to your left
> ➤ Ask them…"You aren't broke are you?"
> ➤ Ask them…"You did get here on time didn't you?"
> ➤ Ask them…"You do have a job don't you?"

- Ask them…"You are filled with the Holy Ghost aren't you?
- Ask them…"You are faithful aren't you?"
- Ask them…"You are paying your tithes aren't you?"
- Ask them…"You didn't have to hitch a ride did you?"

John 15:6-7 NIV If anyone does not remain in me, he is like a branch that is thrown away and withers; such branches are picked up, thrown into the fire and burned. [7] _If you remain in me and my words remain in you, ask whatever you wish, and it will be given you._

17

Get Dressed!!!

Props:
You will need a Police Officer, A doctor, A Baseball Player, A Military Person, and A Road Worker.
*** You will need a "real" police official, and "Military official", but the others can be made up. The Doctor should wear scrubs, a white coat and a stethoscope. The Road worker, can just wear old jeans and t-shirt, work boots, a hard helmet and a orange vest with a orange flag. The ball player may be one of your youth dressed out for ball.
You will also need an armor suit... (FOR THE WHOLE ARMOR OF GOD)

Isaiah 61:1-3 (NIV) The Spirit of the Sovereign LORD is on me, because the LORD has anointed me to preach good news to the poor. He has sent me to bind up the brokenhearted, to proclaim freedom for the captives and release from darkness for the prisoners, [2] to proclaim the year of the Lord's favor and the day of vengeance of our God, to comfort all who mourn, [3] and provide for those who grieve in Zion-- to bestow on them a crown of beauty instead of ashes, the oil of gladness instead of mourning, and a

garment of praise instead of a spirit of despair. They will be called oaks of righteousness, a planting of the LORD for the display of his splendor.

Do you realize that we are often judged by what we have on? Whether we have a job that we have to wear a suit and tie, or if we work at the mall and you have to dress in fashion, or if you work on the roads and wear blue jeans.

HAVE THE ROAD WORKER TO ENTER

When you see a Baseball player... People wear all kinds of stuff...(PUT PICTURES ON THE SCREEN OF FANS IN COSTUMES.) The stands don't go wild until the team in uniform enters the field.

HAVE THE BASEBALL PLAYER COME OUT

When you are sick, it is fine to see the nurse, it is nice to see the receptionist, it is even ok to see the Lab worker... BUT the person that you REALLY want to see is the DOCTOR.

HAVE THE DOCTOR TO COME OUT

When we are battling against terrorism, It is fine to see people out giving their opinions about war, it is ok to hear what Congress is doing, BUT it is an Honor when we see someone among us... fighting for our freedom...

HAVE THE MILITARY WORKER COME OUT

Can you imagine what it would be like to direct traffic in Atlanta in our everyday clothes. It would be impossible as well as an act of suicide.

HAVE THE POLICEMAN TO COME OUT

When you put on a uniform, you get the results of it. Even though, it may be a traffic officer, when he says, "STOP" you stop.

WHY?
> ➢ HE can out run your car…he is on foot!
> ➢ His uniform shows Authority.
> ➢ Some of you are scared, Just because he is here!
> ➢ When you see a police man, you may not be speeding but you slow down.

When you see a policeman, and he tells you to stop:
> ➢ You may not want to stop… but you do.
> ➢ Even if you don't have time to stop…you make time…and stop.
> ➢ Even if you are having a bad day…you stop.
> ➢ Not because of the person…but the uniform that he is wearing.
> ➢ YOU HAVE TO OBEY IT!!!

Matthew 18:18 (NIV)   "I tell you the truth, whatever you bind on earth will be bound in

heaven, and whatever you loose on earth will be loosed in heaven.

The reason it doesn't work for us...lets face it....
- ➢ We speak things out that doesn't come to pass
- ➢ We bind the devil and he beats us down
- ➢ We speak with power and then tuck our tail between our legs and run.

WHY? We have not been fully clothed in the UNIFORM that God has given us!

YOU CAN PUT THIS OFFICER OUT ON OLD DIXIE HWY IN HIS JEANS AND HE WOULD NOT HAVE THE SAME EFFECT THAT HE WOULD IF HE WAS WEARING HIS UNIFORM.

LIKEWISE, WHEN WE ARE NOT CLOTHED IN RIGHTEOUSNESS, THE DEVIL SEES IT FIRST AND WILL WEAR US OUT!!

- ➢ You cant afford to let the devil see you without your uniform
- ➢ He will beat you down
- ➢ Break you up
- ➢ And spit you out

WE HAVE TO WALK IN AUTHORITY!!!

Luke 10:19 (NIV) I have given you authority to trample on snakes and scorpions and to overcome all the power of the enemy; nothing will harm you.

94

2 Corinthians 10:5-8 (NIV) We demolish arguments and every pretension that sets itself up against the knowledge of God, and we take captive every thought to make it obedient to Christ. [6] And we will be ready to punish every act of disobedience, once your obedience is complete. [7] You are looking only on the surface of things. If anyone is confident that he belongs to Christ, he should consider again that we belong to Christ just as much as he. [8] For even if I boast somewhat freely about the authority the Lord gave us for building you up rather than pulling you down, I will not be ashamed of it.

Ephesians 6:10-18 (NIV) Finally, be strong in the Lord and in his mighty power. [11] Put on the full armor of God so that you can take your stand against the devil's schemes. [12] For our struggle is not against flesh and blood, but against the rulers, against the authorities, against the powers of this dark world and against the spiritual forces of evil in the heavenly realms. [13] Therefore put on the full armor of God, so that when the day of evil comes, you may be able to stand your ground, and after you have done everything, to stand. [14] Stand firm then, with the belt of truth buckled around your waist, with the breastplate of righteousness in place, [15] and with your feet fitted with the readiness that comes from the gospel of peace. [16] In addition to all this, take up the shield of faith, with which you can extinguish all the flaming arrows of the evil one. [17] Take the helmet of salvation and the sword of the Spirit, which is the word of God. [18] And pray in the Spirit on all occasions with all kinds of prayers and requests. With this in mind, be alert and always keep on praying for all the saints.

18

GET OUT OF <u>HELL</u> FREE

Props:
You need the "Monopoly Man" (life size) on the platform...Holding a card... "GET OUT OF HELL FREE". Also, it would be great if you had a pit the could look like the pits of hell...flames, screams, fire, smoke...etc...Also, pass out to everyone, Monopoly cards... "GET OUT OF HELL FREE"

Romans 6:22-23 (NIV) But now that you have been set free from sin and have become slaves to God, the benefit you reap leads to holiness, and the result is eternal life. [23] *For the wages of sin is death,* but the gift of God is eternal life in Christ Jesus our Lord.

Luke 16:19-31 (NIV) "There was a rich man who was dressed in purple and fine linen and lived in luxury every day. [20] At his gate was laid a *beggar named Lazarus,* covered with sores [21] and longing to eat what fell from the rich man's table. Even the dogs came and licked his sores. [22] "The time came when the beggar died and the angels carried him to Abraham's side. *The rich man also died* and was buried. **23** *In hell,* where he was in torment, he looked up and saw Abraham far away, with Lazarus by his side. **24** So he called to him, *'Father Abraham, have pity on me and send Lazarus to dip the tip of his finger in water and cool my tongue, because I am in agony in this fire.'* **25** "But Abraham replied, 'Son, remember that in your lifetime you received your good things, while Lazarus received bad things, but now he is comforted here and you are in agony. **26** And besides all this, *between us and you a great chasm has been fixed, so that those who want to go from here to you cannot,* nor can anyone cross over from there to us.' **27** "He answered, 'Then I beg you, father, *send Lazarus to my father's house,* **28** *for I have five brothers. Let him warn them,* so that they will not also come to this place of torment.' **29** "Abraham replied, *'They have Moses and the Prophets;* let them listen to them.' **30** "'No, father Abraham,' he said, 'but *if someone from the dead goes to them, they will repent.'* **31** "He said to him, *'If they do not listen to Moses and the Prophets, they will not be convinced even if someone rises from the dead.'"*

➢ Realize that today…
➢ You have the opportunity to be saved
➢ Tomorrow… you may not
➢ Who may be in hell know…
➢ Wanting you to know… what it is like
➢ The Rich man…even in Hell didn't want his family to come there.

2 Peter 2:4-9 (NIV) For if _God did not spare angels when they sinned, but sent them to hell,_ putting them into gloomy dungeons to be held for judgment; [5] if _he did not spare the ancient world_ when he brought the flood on its ungodly people, but protected Noah, a preacher of righteousness, and seven others; [6] if _he condemned the cities of Sodom and Gomorrah by burning them_ to ashes, and made them an example of what is going to happen to the ungodly; [7] and if he rescued Lot, a righteous man, who was distressed by the filthy lives of lawless men [8] (for that righteous man, living among them day after day, was tormented in his righteous soul by the lawless deeds he saw and heard)-- [9] _if this is so,_ then _the Lord knows how to rescue godly men from trials_ and to _hold the unrighteous for the day of judgment,_ while continuing their punishment.

➤ God gives us the opportunity
➤ NOW....
➤ But once you cross over... it will be TOO LATE
➤ God has mercy on us while we are here, but once our number is called....
➤ Where we go... is where we will stay!!!

Mark 9:43-48 (NIV) _If your hand causes you to sin, cut it off._ It is _better for you to enter life maimed than with two hands to go into hell, where the fire never goes out._ [44] [45] And if your _foot causes you to sin, cut it off. It is better for you to enter life crippled than to have two feet and be thrown into hell._ [46] [47]

And if your eye causes you to sin, pluck it out. It is better for you to enter the kingdom of God with one eye than to have two eyes and be thrown into hell, [48] *where "'their worm does not die, and the fire is not quenched.'*

➤ What in your life is worth going to hell for?
➤ What habit?
➤ What person?
➤ What situation?
➤ What is worth your soul burning in HELL forever and ever?

2 Peter 3:9-14 (NIV) The Lord is not slow in keeping his promise, as some understand slowness. He is patient with you, _not wanting anyone to perish, but everyone to come to repentance._ [10] But the day of the Lord will come like a thief. The heavens will disappear with a roar; the elements will be destroyed by fire, and the earth and everything in it will be laid bare. [11] *Since everything will be destroyed in this way, what kind of people ought you to be? You ought to live holy and godly lives* [12] as you look forward to the day of God and speed its coming. *That day will bring about the destruction of the heavens by _fire_,* and the elements will melt in the heat. [13] But in keeping with his promise we are looking forward to _a new heaven and a new earth, the home of righteousness._ [14] So then, dear friends, since you are looking forward to this, _make every effort to be found spotless, blameless and at peace with him._

➤ MAKE EVERY EFFORT TO BE FOUND … BLAMELESS

JOHN SAYS:

Revelation 20:12-15 (NIV) And I saw the dead, great and small, standing before the throne, and books were opened. Another book was opened, which is _the book of life_. The dead were judged according to what they had done as recorded in the books. [13] The sea gave up the dead that were in it, and death and Hades gave up the dead that were in them, and _each person was judged according to what he had done_. [14] Then death and Hades were thrown into the lake of fire. The lake of fire is the second death. [15] _If anyone's name was not found written in the book of life, he was thrown into the lake of fire._

- ➤ This morning…you have been given an opportunity that many wish they had…
- ➤ An opportunity to get out of "hell" free.
- ➤ If you are here and are not living right
- ➤ Or if you have not confessed Jesus as your Lord and savior…
- ➤ You have the right this morning to "Get out of HELL free" because
- ➤ Jesus Paid the price for you!!!
- ➤ And FOR ME.
- ➤ THIS morning… will you use that card… and by faith step out of your seat and by bringing it down… you are saying YES to JESUS.

I AM SO GLAD… I USED MY 'GET OUT OF HELL FREE' CARD, YEARS AGO…

DON'T WAIT TO LATE...BECAUSE ONCE YOU ARE THERE... YOUR CARD BECOMES VOID!!!

19

Getting God out of the BOX

Prop:
Have a large box on platform with fog machine
and glowing light coming out of it.

To often do we put God in a box… Limiting Him of:

- ➤ His Power
- ➤ His Strength
- ➤ His Willingness
- ➤ His Provision

Matthew 19:26 (NIV) Jesus looked at them and said, "_With man this is impossible_, but _with God ALL things are possible_."

Psalms 147:1-5 (NIV) Praise the LORD. How good it is to sing praises to our God, how pleasant and fitting to praise him! [2] The LORD builds up Jerusalem; he gathers the exiles of Israel. [3] He heals the brokenhearted and binds up their wounds. [4] He determines the number of the stars and calls them each by name. [5] Great is our Lord and mighty in power; _his understanding has no limit._

Ephesians 3:20-21 (NIV) Now to him *who is able to do immeasurably more than all we ask or imagine, according to his power that is at work within us,* [21] to him be glory in the church and in Christ Jesus throughout all generations, for ever and ever! Amen.

LET'S LOOK AT AN EXAMPLE OF "PUTTING JESUS IN A BOX"

Acts 12:5-16 (NIV) … Peter was kept in prison, *but the church was earnestly praying to God for him.* [6] The night before Herod was to bring him to trial, Peter was *sleeping between two soldiers, bound with two chains, and sentries stood guard* at the entrance. [7] Suddenly an angel of the Lord appeared and a light shone in the cell. He struck Peter on the side and woke him up. "Quick, get up!" he said, and the *chains fell off* Peter's wrists. [8] Then the angel said to him, "Put on your clothes and sandals." (TAKE OFF YOUR PRISON CLOTHES... I AM NOT A PRISONER NO MORE... I AM JOINT HEIRS WITH CHRIST) And Peter did so. "Wrap your cloak around you and follow me," the angel told him. [9] Peter followed him *out of the prison,* but he had no idea that what the angel was doing was really happening; he thought he was seeing a vision. [10] They *passed the first and second guards* and came to the iron gate leading to the city. It opened for them by itself, and *they went through it.* When they had walked the length of one street, suddenly the angel left him. [11] Then Peter came to himself and said, "*Now I know without a doubt that the Lord sent his angel and rescued me* from Herod's clutches and from everything the Jewish people were anticipating." [12] When this had dawned on him, *he went to* the house of Mary the mother of John, also called Mark, *where many people had gathered and were praying.* [13] Peter knocked at the outer entrance, and a servant girl named *Rhoda came to answer the door.* [14] When she recognized Peter's voice, *she was so overjoyed she ran back without opening it and exclaimed, "Peter is at the door!"* [15] *"You're out of your mind," they told her.* When she kept insisting that it was so, they said, "It must be his angel." [16] But *Peter kept on knocking, and when they opened the door and saw him, they were astonished.*

➢ IT IS TIME TO GET GOD... OUT OF THE BOX
➢ HE IS BIGGER THAN YOUR BILLS
➢ HE IS BIGGER THAN YOUR PROBLEMS
➢ HE IS BIGGER THAN YOUR SIN
➢ HE IS BIGGER THAN YOUR HABITS
➢ HE IS BIGGER THAN YOUR SUBSTANCE
➢ HE IS BIGGER THAN YOUR LIEING
➢ HE IS BIGGER THAN YOUR GOSSIP
➢ HE IS BIGGER THAN THOSE THAT OPPOSE YOU
➢ HE IS BIGGER THAN THOSE THAT ARE TALKING ABOUT YOU
➢ HE IS BIGGER THAN YOUR EMPLOYER

- ➤ HE IS BIGGER THAN YOUR SICKNESS
- ➤ HE IS BIGGER THAN YOUR MARITAL CONDITION
- ➤ HE IS BIGGER THAN YOUR CHILDREN'S PROBLEMS
- ➤ LET HIM OUT OF THE BOX IN 2006!!!!

MY GOD IS MORE THAN ENOUGH!!!

Matthew 19:26 (NIV) Jesus looked at them and said, _"With man this is impossible, but with God ALL things are possible."_

- ➤ HOW BIG IS YOUR GOD???
- ➤ HOW WEALTHY IS YOUR GOD?
- ➤ HOW DEPENDABLE IS YOUR GOD?
- ➤ HOW LOVING IS YOUR GOD…
- ➤ WITH YOU IT MAY BE IMPOSSIBLE…
- ➤ BUT LET HIM OUT OF THE BOX AND SEE HOW DEPENDABLE HE WILL BE TO YOU!!!!

20

God is BIGGER THAN THAT!!!

Props:
Vending machine with items inside labeled
(fully covering the product)

Healing	Money	Job
Peace	Spouse	Comfort

(You will need them labeled pretty big so you can see them as you purchase them Through the machine.) Don't forget you will need a roll of quarters

You also need a BIG '>' sign and 6 numbers printed on poster board

Too often, do we think that God is this little weak, pansy of a person that can not meet our needs...We pray, but don't receive it, we ask but don't believe it. Let me ask you a simple question: HOW BIG IS YOUR GOD???? YELL IT OUT!!!

WELL let me tell you....

He is BIGGER than that!!!!!!!!!!!!!!

God is Bigger than

- ➢ All my troubles…
- ➢ Bigger than all my fears
- ➢ Bigger than any mountain … that I can or cannot see
- ➢ Bigger than all my heart aches
- ➢ He is bigger trials
- ➢ He is bigger than anything….

In math as I child … we have to draw a Greater than…Less than sign. We would have 2 numbers… and we would have to identify…which was bigger by a symbol. That is still orchestrated in the church … everyday…or at least it should be!! *(have 2 people come on and hold numbers… have someone else place the < toward the right direction.)* Which is greater? The Bigger number is greater…therefore…the small end always opens up to the big number… likewise…we are the small one… God is the Bigger one…that is why we raise our hands in praise to Him. \/ God is BIGGER THAN… BIGGER THAN ANYTHING!!!

Job 33:12 (KJV) … I will answer thee, that God is greater than man.

Psalms 135:5 (NIV) I know that the LORD is great, that our Lord is greater than all gods.

- ➢ We think that He is only there when we need Him

- We have gotten susceptible to convenience…
- We want everything RIGHT NOW
- We stand in front of a micro-wave and tell it to hurry up
- We get our taxes done…and want it back …Instantly…regardless of what it costs us.
- We want instant food when we pull up to a window…
- And yes…we want God instantly …when we get into trouble.

Lets look at an example how some of us use GOD:

You will now unveil a vending machine labeled as GOD

Too often do we think of God like a big ole vending machine…

- Just standing around… waiting to be used
- Just waiting to fulfill our needs
- Just waiting for your request….
- GOD IS BIGGER THAN THAT!!!

John 10:22-30 (NIV) Then came the Feast of Dedication at Jerusalem. It was winter, [23] and Jesus was in the temple area walking in Solomon's Colonnade. [24] The Jews gathered around him, saying, "How long will you keep us in suspense? If you are the Christ, tell us plainly." [25] Jesus answered, "I did tell you, but you do not believe. The miracles I do in

my Father's name speak for me, ²⁶ but you do not believe because you are not my sheep. ²⁷ My sheep listen to my voice; I know them, and they follow me. ²⁸ I give them eternal life, and they shall never perish; no one can snatch them out of my hand. ²⁹ My Father, who has given them to me, *is greater than all ; no one can snatch them out of my Father's hand.* ³⁰ I and the Father are one."

Remember the children of Israel?

They used God like a vending Machine...
They were happy as long as they were satisfied...

> ➤ They wanted delivered and God sent Moses
> ➤ They wanted to cross over... and God divided the water
> ➤ They wanted food... and God sent manna
> ➤ They wanted meat and God sent Quail
> ➤ They wanted clothing... and God wouldn't allow theirs to wear out
> ➤ THEY USED GOD LIKE A VENDING MACHINE..

This is interesting prayer given in Kansas at the opening session of their Senate. It seems prayer still upsets some people. When Minister Joe Wright was asked to open the new session of the Kansas Senate, everyone was expecting the usual generalities, but this is what they heard:

"Heavenly Father, we come before you today to ask your forgiveness and to seek your direction and guidance. We know Your Word says, 'Woe to those who call evil good,' but that is exactly what we have done. We have lost our spiritual equilibrium and reversed our values. We have exploited the poor and called it the lottery. We have rewarded laziness and called it welfare. We have killed our unborn and called it choice. We have shot abortionists and called it justifiable. We have neglected to discipline our children and called it building self esteem. We have abused power and called it politics. We have coveted our neighbor's possessions and called it ambition. We have polluted the air with profanity and pornography and called it freedom of expression. We have ridiculed the time-honored values of our forefathers and called it enlightenment. Search us, Oh, God, and know our hearts today; cleanse us from every sin and set us free. Amen!"

The response was immediate. A number of legislators walked out during the prayer in protest. In 6 short weeks, Central Christian Church, where Rev. Wright is pastor, logged more than 5,000 phone calls with only 47 of those calls responding negatively. The church is now receiving international requests for copies of this prayer from India, Africa and Korea.

Commentator Paul Harvey aired this prayer on his radio program, "The Rest of the Story," and received a larger response to this program than any other he has ever aired.

We must get to the place…that we love God for giving His Son… Not always wanting to use HIM… But to be thankful for what he has already done!!!

21

God will not put more on you than you can stand

Props:
You will need several white pillow cases… on the front, in large letters you need things written on them with bold black marker…. Things that will weigh you down: Lust; Envy; Greed; Family; Friends; Jobs

---

Why do we doubt God????

Doubt is the opposite of faith

Doubt is the negative
Faith is the positive
Why do we rather choose to live in the negative, rather than the positive?

1 Corinthians 10:13 (NIV) No temptation has seized you except what is common to man. And God is faithful; he will not let you be tempted beyond what you can bear. But

when you are tempted, he will also provide a way out so that you can stand up under it.

> ➤ Elijah went through some stuff
> ➤ He saw Gods hand working through it all
> ➤ He found favor with God

In Chapter 16:

> ➤ The King Ahab came against the prophet of God… Elijah
> ➤ The King was worse than all the previous kings of Israel combined.
> ➤ He finally showed his real character by marrying Jezebel
> ➤ He worship Baal

1 Kings 17:1-7 (NIV) Now Elijah the Tishbite, from Tishbe in Gilead, said to Ahab, "As the LORD, the God of Israel, lives, whom I serve, there will be neither dew nor rain in the next few years except at my word." [2] Then the word of the LORD came to Elijah: [3] "Leave here, turn eastward and hide in the Kerith Ravine, east of the Jordan. [4] You will drink from the brook, and I have ordered the ravens to feed you there." [5] So he did what the LORD had told him. He went to the Kerith Ravine, east of the Jordan, and stayed there. [6] The ravens brought him bread and meat in the morning and bread and meat in the evening, and he drank from the brook. [7] Some time later the brook dried up because there had been no rain in the land.

- ➤ We find in chapter 17, verses 8-16 that:
- ➤ God provided a way of survival for him
- ➤ He brought a widow woman to him
- ➤ She didn't have much…but she was willing to share
- ➤ She made him a cake and he did eat.
- ➤ His life was spared. …again

Out of the goodness of this widows heart, she did feed the prophet of God… then her son dies. Vs. 17-23

1 Kings 17:24 (NIV) Then the woman said to Elijah, "Now I know that you are a man of God and that the word of the LORD from your mouth is the truth."

Elijah finally meets with Ahab face to face.
- ➤ Ahab asks Elijah… are you the one bringing havac to Israel
- ➤ Elijah responds…it is not me that is serving a fake God… but the living God.

1 Kings 18:20-21 (NIV) So Ahab sent word throughout all Israel and assembled the prophets on Mount Carmel. 21 Elijah went before the people and said, "How long will you waver between two opinions? If the LORD is God, follow him; but if Baal is God, follow him." But the people said nothing.

> The Prophets of Baal made a sacrifice to Baal, but the sacrifice was not moved
> Elijah offered the sacrifice to the Lord

1 Kings 18:30-40 (NIV) Then Elijah said to all the people, "Come here to me." They came to him, and he repaired the altar of the LORD, which was in ruins. [31] Elijah took twelve stones, one for each of the tribes descended from Jacob, to whom the word of the LORD had come, saying, "Your name shall be Israel." [32] With the stones he built an altar in the name of the LORD, and he dug a trench around it large enough to hold two seahs of seed. [33] He arranged the wood, cut the bull into pieces and laid it on the wood. Then he said to them, "Fill four large jars with water and pour it on the offering and on the wood." [34] "Do it again," he said, and they did it again. "Do it a third time," he ordered, and they did it the third time. [35] The water ran down around the altar and even filled the trench. [36] At the time of sacrifice, the prophet Elijah stepped forward and prayed: "O LORD, God of Abraham, Isaac and Israel, let it be known today that you are God in Israel and that I am your servant and have done all these things at your command. [37] Answer me, O LORD, answer me, so these people will know that you, O LORD, are God, and that you are turning their hearts back again." [38] Then the fire of the LORD fell and burned up the sacrifice, the wood, the stones and the soil, and also licked up the water in the trench. [39] When all the people saw this, they fell

prostrate and cried, "The LORD--he is God! The LORD--he is God!" [40] **Then Elijah commanded them, "Seize the prophets of Baal. Don't let anyone get away!" They seized them, and Elijah had them brought down to the Kishon Valley and slaughtered there.**

After 3 years of draught the rain starting falling

1 Kings 18:41 (NIV) And Elijah said to Ahab, "Go, eat and drink, for there is the sound of a heavy rain."

1 Kings 18:45 (NIV) Meanwhile, the sky grew black with clouds, the wind rose, a heavy rain came....

In chapter 19... we find that Jezebel promises to have Elijah's life by the same time tomorrow.

➢ Elijah gets scared...in the midst of his victory
➢ He runs for his life
➢ He pleads with God... to do what Jezebel has requested
➢ He asks for God to let him lie down and die in his sleep
➢ He was just in his biggest victory
➢ Saw his biggest miracles
➢ Spoke on behalf of God
➢ Was received by God... and now.....

1 Kings 19:4-8 (NIV) while he himself went a day's journey into the desert. He came to a broom tree, sat down under it and prayed that he might die. "I have had enough, LORD," he said. "Take my life; I am no better than my ancestors." ⁵ Then he lay down under the tree and fell asleep.

➢ This shows Elijah's Humanity
➢ He did not fear the King… he feared Jezebel
➢ He was afraid that she would kill him.
➢ He ran for his life
➢ Pleading with God to take him… he thought God put to much on him to bear
➢ When Elijah was in the power of Gods might … he was strong
➢ But in the flesh…he was weak…very weak
➢ Elijah would not die here…because God wasn't done yet… it was only a test
➢ In fact… Elijah would NEVER die, but be 1 of the 2 that never experienced death. (2 Kings 2:11)

⁵… All at once an angel touched him and said, "Get up and eat." ⁶ He looked around, and there by his head was a cake of bread baked over hot coals, and a jar of water. He ate and drank and then lay down again. ⁷ The angel of the LORD came back a second time and touched him and said, "Get up and eat, for the journey is too much for you." ⁸ So he got up and ate and drank. Strengthened by that food, he traveled forty days and forty

nights until he reached Horeb, the mountain of God.

Immediately after this Elijah has an encounter with GOD.

A few chapters later, he would be taken away in a whirl wind, without ever experiencing death.

GOD DOES NOT EXPECT MORE FROM YOU THAN YOU CAN DO!!!
BUT HE DOES EXPECT FROM YOU!!!!

22

HOLD MY ROBE....SO I CAN DANCE!!!

PROPS:
You will need an ark of the covenant, stone 10 commandments, Golden Jar, Rod, AND a robe somewhere up front that you can put on and take off real quick.

Let me tell you what just happened before we pick up our text:

> ➤ The ark of the covenant was being brought into Jerusalem
> ➤ As you know... it was very Holy and Sanctimonious
> ➤ It was not to be touched by Human hands
> ➤ The ark began to fall, as the ox stumbled
> ➤ Uzzah reached out to keep it from falling
> ➤ He died because of his disobedience
> ➤ David became angry at God because of his wrath

THE CONTENTS OF THE ARK:
1. The law of Moses or the Ten Commandments-The old Law
2. Golden Jar of lost Manna- Nutrition
3. Aarons staff that blossomed- Direction

2 Samuel 6:9-13 (NIV) David was afraid of the LORD that day and said, "How can the ark of the LORD ever come to me?" [10] He was not willing to take the ark of the LORD to be with him in the City of David. Instead, he took it aside to the house of Obed-Edom the Gittite. [11] The ark of the LORD remained in the house of Obed-Edom the Gittite for three months, *and the LORD blessed him and his entire household.* **[12] Now King _David was told_, "The LORD has blessed the household of Obed-Edom and everything he has, because of the ark of God."** **So David went down and** *brought up the ark* **of God from the house of Obed-Edom to the City of David** *with rejoicing.* **[13] When those who were carrying the ark of the LORD had taken _six steps_, he sacrificed a bull and a fattened calf.**

➢ David realized that he had to start Praising before the blessing would be delivered.

2 Samuel 6:14 (NIV) _David,_ wearing a linen ephod, danced _before the LORD_ with all his might,

➢ David took off his royal garb made by man…

➤ And danced before the Lord as one of the slaves would
➤ He was in their attire, not the attire of royalty

2 Samuel 6:15 (NIV) while he and the entire house of Israel brought up the ark of the LORD _with shouts and the sound of trumpets._

➤ You have to shout your way to victory…
➤ You have to recall the blessing that God has promised
➤ You have to remember the blessing He has already given

2 Samuel 6:16-17 (NIV) As the ark of the LORD was entering the City of David, Michal daughter of Saul watched from a window. And when _she saw King David leaping and dancing before the LORD, she despised him in her heart._ ¹⁷ They brought the ark of the LORD and set it in its place inside the tent that David had pitched for it, and David sacrificed burnt offerings and fellowship offerings before the LORD.

➤ Not everyone is going to be excited about your promise
➤ Not everyone is going to like it because of your blessing
➤ Not everyone will dance and praise with you

2 Samuel 6:21-22 (NIV) David said to Michal, "It was before the LORD, who chose me rather than your father or anyone from his house when he appointed me ruler over the Lord's people Israel--*I will celebrate before the LORD.* ²² *I will become even more undignified than this, and I will be humiliated in my own eyes.* But by these slave girls you spoke of, I will be held in honor."

> ➢ David let Michal know… it wasn't your father who called me
> ➢ It's not your father that will bless me.
> ➢ You DIDN'T give it to me… and you can't take it away!!

GOD SPEAKS TO DAVID:

2 Samuel 7:9-12 (NIV) *I have been with you wherever you have gone, and I have cut off all your enemies from before you. Now I will make your name great, like the names of the greatest men of the earth.* ¹⁰ And I will provide a place for my people Israel and will plant them so that they can have a home of their own and no longer be disturbed. Wicked people will not oppress them anymore, as they did at the beginning ¹¹ and have done ever since the time I appointed leaders over my people Israel. *I will also give you rest from all your enemies.* "'The LORD declares to you that *the LORD himself will establish a house for you:* ¹² When your days are over and you rest with your fathers, *I will raise up your offspring to succeed you,* who

will come from your own body, and I will establish his kingdom.

➤ God speaks to David and says:
➤ I have been moving from place to place with a tent as my dwelling (7:6)
➤ But I have chosen you, to make your name great, like the names of the greatest men on earth. (7:9)
➤ In verse 11, God declares that He will establish a House for David
➤ A permanent place…. (WE ARE THE TEMPLE OF THE HOLY GHOST)
➤ In verse 12, God promised David that he will bless his offspring and they shall succeed.

2 Samuel 8:6 (NIV) … *The LORD gave David victory wherever he went.*

2 Samuel 8:14 (NIV) … *The LORD gave David victory wherever he went.*

DAVID HAD TO LEARN TO PRAISE GOD…RIGHT WHERE HE WAS….

David received his blessing after he obeyed and allowed the Ark into the City of David….

God wants to bless you… but you have to allow Him in

God is wanting you to be excited about your relationship with him.

> ➢ *WE ARE NO LONGER UNDER THE LAW…BUT GRACE*
> ➢ *WE ARE NO LONGER STUCK WITH JUST MANNA*
> ➢ *WE ARE NO LONGER TRAPPED BY SOMEONE ELSE LEADING US… THE VEIL WAS RENT THAT I COULD GO BOLDLY BEFORE THE THRONE….*

I WILL PRAISE HIM…… EVEN IF KNOW ONE ELSE WILL!!!!

23

HOLD ON TO IT!!!

Props:
You will need a boxing ring 12x12-5 feet tall. 2 pairs of boxing gloves

In Genesis 32:1-21, we find the story of Jacob preparing to meet with his brother Esau, years after the deception of stealing the family inheritance and blessing.

Genesis 32:22-24 (NIV) That night Jacob got up and took his two wives, his two maidservants and his eleven sons and crossed the ford of the Jabbok. [23] After he had sent them across the stream, he sent over all his possessions. [24] So Jacob was left alone,

1.) Some places you go…you have to go alone… in the dark of the night
   a. Sometimes it is prayer
   b. Sometimes it is in your trials
   c. Sometimes it is in while you are in your valley

d. BUT Praise GOD... He promises never to leave us nor forsake us. (Deut 31:6)

...and a man wrestled with him till daybreak.

2.) Sometime you have to press your way through
   a. Peniel was not only the place know for the face of God... but also
   b. A place to wrestle with God.
   c. Sometime you are up all night ... twisting and turning... up and down... wrestling with God.
   d. Sometimes you have to roll around fighting and kicking... to keep your mind and to keep your family, to keep your children , to keep your marriage.

Genesis 32:25 (NIV) When the man saw that he could not overpower him,

3.) Jacob was determined not to give up
   a. When Jacob was attacked... all the sudden something rose up in him
   b. When you finally get enough... something will rise up in you!!!
   c. Something will start pour out of you in authority
   d. Boldness....HOLY boldness will be revealed...
   e. Therefore ... Jacob began to over take the one he was wrestling with.

Genesis 32:25 (NIV)...he touched the socket of Jacob's hip so that his hip was wrenched as he wrestled with the man. [26] Then the man said, "Let me go, for it is daybreak."

4.) God will give you a way out.
   a. Be careful what you pray for.
   b. Be careful what you say.
   c. Jacob was given the opportunity to let go
   d. Jacob was given the opportunity to blessed or to be cursed.
   e. Even with a hip out of sock... he wouldn't give up
   f. Nor would he let go...

JACOB WOULD BE CRIPPLED THE REST OF HIS LIFE...BUT IT WOULD BE A CONSTANT REMINDER....OF HIS NEW ROYALTY WITH GOD.

DON'T LET GO OF YOU BLESSING...HOLD ON TO IT!!!!

But Jacob replied, "I will not let you go unless you bless me."

5.) Jacob had been up all night
   a. He was all alone
   b. He was tired from his battle
   c. He was wounded

129

d. He could have very easily given up…
BUT .. .HE SAID
e. I am not leaving here without my
blessing….

WHAT WOULD HAPPEN IF YOU
DEMANDED YOUR BLESSING???? You deserve
it… it belongs to you… WHY NOT GET WHAT
IS COMING TO YOU?

Genesis 32:27-30 (NIV) The man asked him, "What is your name?" "Jacob," he answered. [28] Then the man said, "Your name will no longer be Jacob, but Israel,(Israel means…he who strives with GOD…or he who perseveres.) because _you have struggled with God and with men and have overcome."_ [29] Jacob said, "Please tell me your name." But he replied, "Why do you ask my name?" _Then he blessed him there._ [30] So Jacob called the place Peniel, saying, _"It is because I saw God face to face, and yet my life was spared._

Peniel= *Face of God*

Peniel was also the "*place to wrestle with God*"

While most of us will never PHYSICALLY wrestle with God… we can
   1. Seek Him earnestly in prayer
   2. Confess our sins and ask for forgiveness

130

3. *Hunger and thirst after his kingdom and intimate presence*
4. *Desire the power of the Holy Spirit*
5. *Pursue a life of true faith and righteousness*

We find in the next chapter ... Chapter 33, after Jacob had wrestled with God ALL night...after his hip was thrown out of socket... after he used up all his strength and energy... Jacob looked up... and there was ESAU.

Genesis 33:4 (NIV)   But Esau ran to meet Jacob and embraced him; he threw his arms around his neck and kissed him. And they wept.

WHAT ARE YOU WAITING FOR... GOD IS STANDING WITH HIS ARMS OUTSTRETCHED FOR YOU!!!!

24

Holy Heifers

Props:
You will need several cows on the platform with me. You will also need several black spots with white writing….. "I am not a Holy Heifer" Hosea 4:16- To pass out for the congregation.

Last week we covered the sin of "Gossip". This week, I want to go a step further. I am going to take about 4 weeks talking about … "Church Sins" things that we know are sin but accept. We know that if you are an:

> ➢ Alcoholic that God can deliver you
> ➢ A drug addict God can set you free
> ➢ We believe that there will come a time that you will no longer desire those things
> ➢ BUT what about the things we just accept?

This morning I want to take us to the "Second Church Sin"

THE SIN OF STUBBORNESS

Hosea 4:16 (NIV) *The Israelites are stubborn, like a stubborn heifer.* **How then can the LORD pasture them like lambs in a meadow?**

The question that is asked in Hosea is:

- ➢ How can God lead those that don't want to be lead
- ➢ How can you make someone grow that don't want to grow
- ➢ How can you make someone faithful that doesn't want to be faithful
- ➢ It is easy to pasture and lead sheep than it is to:
- ➢ Lead and pasture Holy Heifers (Someone who just wants to be difficult)

Isaiah 46:9-13 (NIV) **Remember the former things, those of long ago; I am God, and there is no other; I am God, and there is none like me.** **10** **I make known the end from the beginning, from ancient times, what is still to come. I say: My purpose will stand, and I will do all that I please.** **11** **From the east I summon a bird of prey; from a far-off land, a man to fulfill my purpose.** ***What I have said, that will I bring about;*** **what I have planned, that will I do.** **12** ***Listen to me, you stubborn-hearted,*** **you who are far from righteousness.** **13** **I am bringing my righteousness near, it is not far away; and my salvation will not be delayed. I will grant salvation to Zion, my splendor to Israel.**

Isaiah 48:1-6 (NIV) "Listen to this, O house of Jacob, you who are called by the name of Israel and come from the line of Judah, you who take oaths in the name of the LORD and invoke the God of Israel-- but not in truth or righteousness-- ² you who call yourselves citizens of the holy city and rely on the God of Israel-- the LORD Almighty is his name: ³ *I foretold the former things long ago, my mouth announced them and I made them known; then suddenly I acted, and they came to pass.* ⁴ For *I knew how stubborn you were;* the sinews of your neck were iron, your forehead was bronze. ⁵ Therefore I told you these things long ago; before they happened I announced them to you so that you could not say, 'My idols did them; my wooden image and metal god ordained them.' ⁶ You have heard these things; look at them all. Will you not admit them? *"From now on I will tell you of new things, of hidden things unknown to you.*

➢ God wants to show us mysteries
➢ He wants to show us sign and wonders
➢ BUT He can not if we are STUBBORN.

Jeremiah 5:21-25 (NIV) Hear this, you foolish and senseless people, who have eyes but do not see, who have ears but do not hear: ²² Should you not fear me?" declares the LORD. "Should you not tremble in my presence? I made the sand a boundary for the sea, an everlasting barrier it cannot cross. The waves may roll, but they cannot prevail; they may roar, but they cannot cross it. ²³ *But these people have stubborn and rebellious hearts;* they have turned aside and gone away. ²⁴ They do not say to themselves, 'Let us fear the LORD our God, who gives autumn and spring rains in season, who assures us of the regular weeks of harvest.' ²⁵ *Your wrongdoings have kept these away; your sins have deprived you of good.*

➢ Stubbornness deprives you from God's blessings
➢ Stubbornness keep a argument fueled
➢ Stubbornness causes marriages to end
➢ Stubbornness keeps a man from eating

Mark 16:14-19 (NIV) Later Jesus appeared to the Eleven as they were eating; _he rebuked them for their lack of faith and their stubborn refusal to believe_ those who had seen him after he had risen. ¹⁵ He said to them, "Go into all the world and preach the good news to all creation. ¹⁶ Whoever believes and is baptized will be saved, but whoever does not believe will be condemned. ¹⁷ And these signs will accompany those who believe: In my name they will drive out demons; they will speak in new tongues; ¹⁸ they will pick up snakes with their hands; and when they drink deadly poison, it will not hurt them at all; they will place their hands on sick people, and they will get well." ¹⁹ After the Lord Jesus had spoken to them, he was taken up into heaven and he sat at the right hand of God.

Many say that they are not giving their heart to the Lord:

- ➢ Because my wife thinks this is what I need
- ➢ This is what my parents want me to do
- ➢ This is what the church is trying to persuade me in

BUT the Bible says that ALL of us was made to commune with God. That is our purpose, and that is our destiny!!! ALL OF US. We at least have that in common.

25

I need a hook up

"I MESSED IT UP...BUT GOD HOOKED IT UP!"

➤ How many of you have ever needed.... A HOOK UP???

➤ How many of you has God ever ...HOOKED UP???

Genesis 16:1-5 (NIV)   Now Sarai, Abram's wife, had borne him no children. But she had an Egyptian maidservant named Hagar; ² so she said to Abram, "The LORD has kept me from having children. Go, sleep with my maidservant; perhaps I can build a family through her." Abram agreed to what Sarai said. ³ So after Abram had been living in Canaan ten years, Sarai his wife took her Egyptian maidservant Hagar and gave her to her husband to be his wife. ⁴ He slept with Hagar, and she conceived. When she knew she was pregnant, she began to despise her mistress. ⁵ Then Sarai said to Abram, "You are responsible for the wrong I am suffering. I put my servant in your arms, and now that she knows she is pregnant, she despises

me. May the LORD judge between you and me."

Genesis 17:17-21 (NIV) Abraham fell facedown; he laughed and said to himself, "Will a son be born to a man a hundred years old? Will Sarah bear a child at the age of ninety?" [18] And Abraham said to God, "If only Ishmael might live under your blessing!" [19] Then God said, "Yes, but your wife Sarah will bear you a son, and you will call him Isaac. I will establish my covenant with him as an everlasting covenant for his descendants after him. [20] And as for Ishmael, I have heard you: I will surely bless him; I will make him fruitful and will greatly increase his numbers. He will be the father of twelve rulers, and I will make him into a great nation. [21] But my covenant I will establish with Isaac, whom Sarah will bear to you by this time next year."

➤ God had a plan for Abram's life…but HE MESSED IT UP
➤ How many of you all have had a calling on your life… but
➤ You ultimately messed it up…
➤ Even in the midst of our mess …
➤ God has a way of HOOKING US UP….
➤ After we have messed things up in our life….isn't great to know that God still loves us so much that He will still give us the "HOOK UP!"

Luke 15:11-20 (NIV) Jesus continued: "There was a man who had two sons. [12] The younger one said to his father, 'Father, give me my share of the estate.' So he divided his property between them. [13] "Not long after that, the younger son got together all he had, set off for a distant country and there squandered his wealth in wild living. [14] After he had spent everything, there was a severe famine in that whole country, and he began to be in need. [15] So he went and hired himself out to a citizen of that country, who sent him to his fields to feed pigs. [16] He longed to fill his stomach with the pods that the pigs were eating, but no one gave him anything. [17] _**"When he came to his senses**_**, he said, 'How many of my father's hired men have food to spare, and here I am starving to death! [18] I will set out and go back to my father and say to him: Father, I have sinned against heaven and against you. [19] I am no longer worthy to be called your son; make me like one of your hired men.' [20] So he got up and went to his father. "But while he was still a long way off,** _**his father saw him and was filled with compassion for him; he ran to his son, threw his arms around him and kissed him.**_

THINK ABOUT YOUR LIFE:
- ➤ You got on drugs….you messed up
- ➤ BUT God got you off and now you have a testimony…God hooked you up!!
- ➤ You went through a divorce … you messed up…

- BUT God forgave you and put you in ministry…God hooked you up.
- You made a mess out of your finances…. You messed up…
- BUT God still made you debt free…God hooked you up.
- HOW MANY OF YOU ALL HAVE EVER HAD A 'HOOK UP'
- HOW MANY OF YOU ALL STILL NEED A 'HOOK UP'?

Let's look at one more example…of God hooking someone up…

Numbers 20:7-12 (NIV) The LORD said to Moses, [8] "Take the staff, and you and your brother Aaron gather the assembly together. Speak to that rock before their eyes and it will pour out its water. You will bring water out of the rock for the community so they and their livestock can drink." [9] So Moses took the staff from the Lord's presence, just as he commanded him. [10] He and Aaron gathered the assembly together in front of the rock and Moses said to them, "Listen, you rebels, must we bring you water out of this rock?" [11] Then Moses raised his arm and struck the rock twice with his staff. Water gushed out, and the community and their livestock drank. [12] But the LORD said to Moses and Aaron, "Because you did not trust in me enough to honor me as holy in the sight of the Israelites, you will not bring this community into the land I give them."

- Moses messed up...he smote the rock...instead of talking to it...
- Moses truly did mess up...
- Because of that...we remember the last part of Moses life....
- He didn't get to go into the promised land...
- What a shame...
- We leave the story there....
- Moses messed up and it was over...
- BUT WAS IT...
- Lets read....

Deuteronomy 34:5-7 (NIV) And Moses the servant of the LORD died there in Moab, as the LORD had said. [6] He buried him in Moab, in the valley opposite Beth Peor, but to this day no one knows where his grave is. [7] Moses was a hundred and twenty years old when he died, yet his eyes were not weak nor his strength gone.

- After Moses messed up...
- We find out that God still 'hooked him up'
- The Bible says that God... personally buried him...
- Now that is a HOOK UP!!!
- No one to this day can find him...
- I would say that Moses got the HOOK UP...
- MOSES finished well!!!

Up need a hook up?? I know the man that can do it!!!

26

In Recovery

Props:
You need the Platform set up with Hospital
items: A hospital bed... surgery cart...etc...

1 Samuel 30:3-6 (NIV) When David and his men came to Ziklag, they found it destroyed by fire and their wives and sons and daughters taken captive. [4] So David and his men wept aloud until they had no strength left to weep. [5] David's two wives had been captured--Ahinoam (of Jezreel) and Abigail, (the widow of Nabal of Carmel.) [6] David was greatly distressed because the men were talking of stoning him; each one was bitter in spirit because of his sons and daughters. _But David found strength in the LORD his God._

One day...David had it all...
The next day...everything seemed to be taken from him

> ➤ He lost all his possessions
> ➤ He lost his buildings
> ➤ He lost his sons

> He lost his daughters
> He lost his wives

BUT

DAVID FOUND FAVOR

1 Samuel 30:8-10 (NIV) and *David inquired of the LORD*, "Shall I pursue this raiding party? Will I overtake them?" *"Pursue them,"* he answered. *"You will certainly overtake them and succeed in the rescue."* [9] David and the six hundred men with him came to the Besor Ravine, where some stayed behind, [10] for *two hundred men were too exhausted* to cross the ravine. *But David and four hundred men continued* the pursuit.

> David had to battle what was his
> David had to pursue what rightfully belonged to him
> We must battle the devil for what is ours
> We give up so easily
> Our family
> Our church
> Our finances

1 Samuel 30:17-20 (NIV) David fought them from dusk until the evening of the next day,

and none of them got away, except four hundred young men who rode off on camels and fled. [18] *David recovered everything* the Amalekites had taken, including his two wives. [19] *Nothing was missing:* young or old, boy or girl, plunder or anything else they had taken. David brought everything back. [20] He took all the flocks and herds, and his men drove them ahead of the other livestock, saying, "This is David's plunder."

WHEN YOU ARE IN RECOVERY IN THE HOSPITAL:

➤ The test is over
➤ The surgery is complete
➤ The worst is behind you
➤ Healing begins within you.
➤ God has to do the final healing process that Doctors can not do

2 Kings 1:1-4 (NIV) After Ahab's death, Moab rebelled against Israel. [2] Now Ahaziah had fallen through the lattice of his upper room in Samaria and injured himself. So he sent messengers, saying to them, "Go and consult Baal-Zebub, the god of Ekron, to see if I will recover from this injury." [3] But the angel of the LORD said to Elijah the Tishbite, "Go up and meet the messengers of the king of Samaria and ask them, *'Is it because there is no God in Israel that you are going off to consult Baal-Zebub,* the god of Ekron?' [4] Therefore this is what the LORD says: *'You will not leave the bed you are lying on. You will certainly die!'"* So Elijah went.

➢ We must understand… God is the giver of good gifts

James 1:17 (NIV) Every good and perfect gift is from above, coming down from the Father of the heavenly lights, who does not change like shifting shadows.

➢ We must also understand that rejecting Gods will is death.

Romans 6:23 (NIV) For the wages of sin is death, but the gift of God is eternal life in Christ Jesus our Lord.

27

In the Desert But NOT deserted!!!!

PROPS:
YOU NEED A SPACE 12X12 ON THE
PLATFORM...FIXED UP LIKE A DESERT---
Cactus's -tumble weeds-sand- big rock...

Psalms 63:1 (NIV) A psalm of David. When he was in the Desert of Judah. O God, you are my God, earnestly I seek you; _my soul thirsts_ _for you, my body longs for you, in a dry and_ _weary land where there is no water._

➤ How many of you have ever been in a dry land?
➤ How many of you have ever felt left behind?
➤ How many of you have ever felt that God was a million miles away?

Deuteronomy 31:8 (NIV) The LORD himself goes before you and will be with you; _he will_ _never leave you nor forsake you. Do not be_ _afraid; do not be discouraged."_

- ➤ NOTICE: He never said…you will never go through anything
- ➤ He did not say that you would never slip nor stumble
- ➤ He never said you wouldn't question your whereabouts.

Exodus 16:1-14 (NIV) The whole Israelite community set out from Elim and came to the Desert of Sin, which is between Elim and Sinai, on the fifteenth day of the second month after they had come out of Egypt. [2] *In the desert the whole community grumbled against Moses and Aaron.* [3] *The Israelites said to them, "If only we had died by the Lord's hand in Egypt! There we sat around pots of meat and ate all the food we wanted,* **but you have brought us out into this desert to starve this entire assembly to death."** [4] **Then the LORD said to Moses,** *"I will rain down bread from heaven for you. The people* **are to go out each day and gather enough for that day.** *In this way I will test them and see whether they will follow my instructions.* [5] **On the sixth day they are to prepare what they bring in, and that is to be twice as much as they gather on the other days."** [6] **So Moses and Aaron said to all the Israelites, "In the evening you will know that it was the LORD who brought you out of Egypt,** [7] **and in the morning you will see the glory of the LORD, because** *he has heard your grumbling against him.* **Who are we, that you should grumble against us?"** [8] **Moses also said,** *"You will know that it was the LORD when he*

150

gives you meat to eat in the evening and all the bread you want in the morning, because he has heard your grumbling against him. Who are we? You are not grumbling against us, but against the LORD." [9] Then Moses told Aaron, "Say to the entire Israelite community, 'Come before the LORD, for he has heard your grumbling.'" [10] While Aaron was speaking to the whole Israelite community, *they looked toward the desert, and there was the glory of the LORD appearing in the cloud.* [11] The LORD said to Moses, [12] "I have heard the grumbling of the Israelites. Tell them, *'At twilight you will eat meat, and in the morning you will be filled with bread. Then you will know that I am the LORD your God.'"* [13] That evening quail came and covered the camp, and in the morning there was a layer of dew around the camp. [14] When the dew was gone, *thin flakes like frost on the ground* appeared on the desert floor.

- ➢ Even in all of our complaining….HE hears us
- ➢ Even in all of our nagging….HE hears us
- ➢ Even when we don't deserve it…HE hears us
- ➢ Even when we are in the desert….HE IS WITH US!!!

Matthew 8:23-27 (NIV) Then Jesus got into the boat and his disciples followed him. [24] Without warning, a furious storm came up on the lake, so that the *waves swept over the boat.* But Jesus was sleeping. [25] The disciples went and woke him, saying, "Lord, save us! We're going to drown!" [26] He replied, "You of little faith, why are you so afraid?" *Then he got up and rebuked the winds and the waves, and it was completely calm.* [27] The men were amazed and asked, "What kind of man is this? *Even the winds and the waves obey him!*"

- ➢ God is the God of the mountain
- ➢ He is also the God of the valley
- ➢ He is the God of the Garden of Beauty
- ➢ He is also the God of the desert
- ➢ HE is the God of steams of living water
- ➢ He is also the God of the stormy sea
- ➢ He is the God when you are rich
- ➢ He is also the God when you are broke
- ➢ He is the God when all is well
- ➢ He is also the God when all hell breaks loose….
- ➢ HE IS GOD!!!!

Isaiah 45:1-3 (NIV) "This is what the LORD says to his anointed, (to Cyrus, whose right hand I take hold of to subdue nations before him and to strip kings of their armor, to open doors before him so that gates will not be shut) [2] I will go before you and will level the mountains; I will break down gates of bronze and cut through bars of iron. [3] I will give you the treasures of darkness, riches stored in secret places, so that you may know that I am the LORD, the God of Israel, who summons you by name.

THIS IS WHAT THE LORD SAYS TO HIS
ANOINTED.......
   a. I will go before you
   b. I will level YOUR mountains.
   c. I will break down the gates of Hell in your
      life.
   d. I will cut through bars of iron for you.
   e. I will give you the treasures of the wicked
   f. I will give you riches stored up in secret
      places.
   g. I will do this so that you may know that I am
      your GOD!!

28

IN THE EYE OF THE STORM

Props:
You will need a storm CD...Thunder and rain, lightning flashes in the sanctuary. The Choir could sing, "Mercy and Grace" to a slide show presentation of Mobile Alabama's Hurricane Relief (or the 911 New York tragedy) The choir can sing in the midst of your sermon...towards the end.
***You need and old boat... beaten and battered....

After Jesus fed the multitude of 5000, he sent his disciples ahead of him...

Matthew 14:22-27 (KJV)   And straightway Jesus constrained his disciples to get into a ship, and to go before him unto the other side, while he sent the multitudes away. [23] And when he had sent the multitudes away,

he went up into a mountain apart to pray: and when the evening was come, he was there alone. [24] But the ship was now *in the midst of the sea,* tossed with waves: for the wind was contrary. [25] And in the fourth watch of the night Jesus went unto them, walking on the sea. [26] And when the disciples saw him walking on the sea, they were troubled, saying, It is a spirit; and they cried out for fear. [27] But straightway Jesus spake unto them, saying, *Be of good cheer; it is I; be not afraid.*

IN THE MIDST

- ➤ The MIDST is between the point of Departure and the Point of Arrival!!!
- ➤ God ALWAYS shows up in the "MIDST"

Psalms 46:1-3 (KJV) ... *God is our refuge and strength, a very present help in trouble.* [2] **Therefore will not we fear, though the earth be removed, and** *though the mountains be carried into the midst of the sea;* [3] *Though the waters thereof roar and be troubled,* **though the mountains shake with the swelling thereof. Selah.**

Psalms 107:29 (KJV) He maketh the storm a calm, so that the waves thereof are still.

- ➤ As Sherry said Wednesday "What is over your head…is under God's feet!

156

Isaiah 43:1-3 (KJV) But now thus saith the LORD that created thee, O Jacob, and he that formed thee, O Israel, Fear not: for I have redeemed thee, I have called thee by thy name; thou art mine. [2] *When thou passest through the waters, I will be with thee;* and *through the rivers, they shall not overflow thee:* when thou walkest through the fire, thou shalt not be burned; neither shall the flame kindle upon thee. [3] For I am the LORD thy God, the Holy One of Israel, thy Saviour...

AFTER JESUS HAD MINISTERED TO THE MULTITUDES:

Mark 4:35-39 (KJV) And the same day, when the even was come, he saith unto them, Let us pass over unto the other side. [36] And when they had sent away the multitude, they took him even as he was in the ship. And there were also with him other little ships. [37] And *there arose a great storm of wind, and the waves beat into the ship, so that it was now full.* [38] And he was in the hinder part of the ship, asleep on a pillow: and they awake him, and say unto him, Master, carest thou not that we perish? [39] And he arose, and rebuked the wind, and said unto the sea, *Peace, be still.* And *the wind ceased*, and *there was a great calm.*

Psalms 124:2-5 (NIV) ...*if the LORD had not been on our side* when men attacked us, {3} when their anger flared against us, they would have swallowed us alive; [4] *the flood would have engulfed us, the torrent would have swept over us,* [5] the raging waters would have swept us away.

IF IT HAD NOT BEEN FOR THE LORD!!!!!

29

Is the DOCTOR in?

Props:
You need a doctor outfit- Possible scrubs and a white Dr. Coat to preach in.
Have a skit with some doctors and nurses, where they are so busy tending to each other and socializing that the patient dies. There will be gun shot victims, aids patients etc.- The doctors and nurses will be pre-occupied on the phones, watching TV, simply, NOT DOING THEIR JOB!

Matthew 9:9-13 (NIV) As Jesus went on from there, he saw a man named Matthew sitting at the tax collector's booth. "Follow me," he told him, and Matthew got up and followed him. [10] While Jesus was having dinner at Matthew's house, many tax collectors and "sinners" came and ate with him and his disciples. [11] When the Pharisees saw this, they asked his disciples, "Why does your teacher eat with tax collectors and 'sinners'?" [12] On hearing this, Jesus said, _"It is not the healthy who need a doctor, but the sick._ [13] But go and learn what this means: 'I

desire mercy, not sacrifice.' For I have not come to call the righteous, but sinners."

➢ God has called up to be doctors to the spiritually sick

Galatians 6:1-2 (NIV) Brothers, if someone is caught in a sin, you _who are spiritual_ should _restore him_ gently. But watch yourself, or you also may be tempted. ² _Carry each other's burdens,_ and in this way you will fulfill the law of Christ.

➢ When you see someone one with crutches…you help them carry things…
➢ If you see someone in a wheel chair… you push them
➢ The same goes spiritually…if you see some lusting…you steer them the right direction
➢ If you see someone sinning…you encourage them to get close to Jesus…
➢ We don't just push them to the side.

Luke 15:4-6 (NIV) "Suppose one of you has a hundred sheep and loses one of them. Does he not _leave the ninety-nine_ in the open country and _go after the lost sheep_ until he finds it? ⁵ And when he finds it, he joyfully puts it on his shoulders ⁶ and goes home. Then he calls his friends and neighbors together and says, 'Rejoice with me; I have found my lost sheep.'

SKIT TEAM WILL COME IN HERE...ABOUT 3 MINUTES- ALL LIGHTS GO OUT... AND EVERYTHING FOCUS'S ON CETNER STAGE.

- ➢ What is wrong with this picture?
- ➢ We get upset when we go to the doctors office and we don't get service
- ➢ What kind of service are we offering our wounded?
- ➢ In the church, sinners come in dying week after week
- ➢ We are more concerned about positions and issues that just don't matter
- ➢ Fighting each other
- ➢ Too busy to even notice that the person sitting beside us is bleeding to death while we sit in our own little world
- ➢ Our calling is to give the sick and lost a dose of penicillin/the Word of God that will cure all the ales them.
- ➢ God is the source of healing...we are just the instrument used.
- ➢ The doctor has several instruments, but he is the one in control.
- ➢ He will use the hammer to tap on your knee...to see your reflex
- ➢ He will use a stick to press your tongue down to see your throat
- ➢ He will use a stethoscope to put near your heart to hear its beat

➢ Those are all instruments that the doctor uses…He could check you without the instrument…but he chooses to use them….

➢ GOD CHOSES TO USE YOU!!!

James 5:13 (NIV) Is any one of you in _trouble? He should pray._ Is anyone _happy? Let him sing_ songs of praise.

James 5:14-15 (NIV) Is any one of you sick? He should call the elders of the church to _pray over him and anoint him with oil_ in the name of the Lord. [15] And the prayer offered in faith will make the sick person well; the Lord will raise him up. If he has sinned, he will be forgiven.

Luke 15:7 (NIV) I tell you that in the same way there will be more rejoicing in heaven over _one sinner_ who repents than over _ninety-nine righteous persons who do not need to repent._

➢ It is time that we put on our spiritual scrubs and get busy

➢ Doing the Fathers will

➢ Taking the captive and setting them free

➢ Healing the Sick

➢ Delivering the possessed

➢ And Saving the Lost

30

Is the Doctor in?
"Part 2"

Do a brief overview from last sermon

Props:
You need a doctor coat and stethoscope again.
On the platform...some doctor equipment. You need:
A heart; A Brain; Ear; Nose; Eye

Matthew 9:9-13 (NIV) As Jesus went on from there, he saw a man named Matthew sitting at the tax collector's booth. "Follow me," he told him, and Matthew got up and followed him. [10] While Jesus was having dinner at Matthew's house, many tax collectors and "sinners" came and ate with him and his disciples. [11] When the Pharisees saw this, they asked his disciples, "Why does your teacher eat with tax collectors and 'sinners'?" [12] On hearing this, Jesus said, _"It is not the healthy who need a doctor, but the sick._ [13] But go and learn what this means: 'I desire mercy, not sacrifice.' For I have not come to call the righteous, but sinners."

Last week… we saw an emergency room…where the nurses and doctors were preoccupied to care for the patients…therefore they died. We compared that to the church…that we have people coming in wounded, sick and desperate, yet we don't even notice because we are to preoccupied with our selves.

Today I want to conclude this message…. Is there a Doctor in the house?

There are all kinds of doctors, let's take a look at a few:

Optometrist- One who studies the eye

Mark 9:47-48 (NIV) And if your eye causes you to sin, pluck it out. It is better for you to enter the kingdom of God with one eye than to have two eyes and be thrown into hell, [48] where "'their worm does not die, and the fire is not quenched.'

> ➤ Our eyes wonder …where they shouldn't be wandering
> ➤ Our eyes can get us in trouble
> ➤ They can be sharp and cut through someone

- You can read some ones soul…through their eyes
- Be careful when someone cant look at you in the eye when talking
- The eye can flirt
- The eye can cry

ENT- Ear, Nose and Throat Doctor

Proverbs 18:21 (NIV) The tongue has the power of life and death….

- What gets us into trouble more than anything else?
- Our mouth!!!
- We need to guard our mouth
- And be careful to what we listen to!

Philippians 4:8 (NIV) Finally, brothers, whatever is true, whatever is noble, whatever is right, whatever is pure, whatever is lovely, whatever is admirable--if anything is excellent or praiseworthy--think about such things.

Acts 2:26 (NIV) Therefore my heart is glad and my tongue rejoices; my body also will live in hope,

Cardiologist- A Heart Doctor

➢ Some of us need a heart doctor
➢ Because our heart has gotten hard
➢ Our heart has been corrupt with hatred, jealousy, and strife
➢ Our heart needs to be pure

Ezekiel 36:26 (NIV) I will give you a new heart and put a new spirit in you; I will remove from you your heart of stone and give you a heart of flesh.

Psalms 24:4-5 (NIV) He who has clean hands and a pure heart, who does not lift up his soul to an idol or swear by what is false. [5] He will receive blessing from the LORD and vindication from God his Savior.

➢ God promises to restore Israel
➢ Not only Physically, but Spiritually as well
➢ This restoration involves giving them a new heart that is as tender as tender as flesh.
➢ Giving them the power to respond to God's word.

Psychologist- One that studies the mind

Romans 12:2 (NIV)   Do not conform any longer to the pattern of this world, but be transformed by the renewing of your mind. Then you will be able to test and approve what God's will is--his good, pleasing and perfect will.

Isaiah 26:3-4 (NIV) God will keep in perfect peace him whose mind is steadfast, because he trusts in you. ⁴ Trust in the LORD forever, for the LORD, the LORD, is the Rock eternal.

- ➢ All sins starts in the mind
- ➢ The battlefield is our mind
- ➢ In fact…the gates of hell is represented by our mind

Dermatologist- Skin Doctor

Ephesians 6:11-13 (NIV)   Put on the full armor of God so that you can take your stand against the devil's schemes. ¹² For our struggle is not against flesh and blood, but against the rulers, against the authorities, against the powers of this dark world and against the spiritual forces of evil in the

heavenly realms. [13] Therefore put on the full armor of God, so that when the day of evil comes, you may be able to stand your ground, and after you have done everything, to stand.

- ➤ We have way to many problems in the FLESH
- ➤ Some of our skin is too…..SENSITIVE
- ➤ Any little thing gets under your SKIN
- ➤ We must develop…tough SKIN

WHAT KIND OF DOCTOR DO YOU NEED AN APPOINTMENT WITH??

DOCTOR JESUS CAN FIX ANYTHING…. YOU HAVE TO BE WILLING TO LET HIM!!

31

It is what it is....
But it is not what it
looks like!!!!

Children of Israel were facing the
sea...
It is what it is...but it is not what
it looks like...

➢ The children of Israel was fleeing for their
life.
➢ Pharaoh had finally released them...but then
changed his mind.
➢ He sent his army to stop them from
crossing the Red Sea.

Exodus 14:9-12 (NIV)   The Egyptians--all
Pharaoh's horses and chariots, horsemen
and troops--pursued the Israelites and
overtook them as they camped by the sea
near Pi Hahiroth, opposite Baal Zephon. [10] **As**
Pharaoh approached, the Israelites looked

up, and there were the Egyptians, marching after them. They were terrified and cried out to the LORD. [11] They said to Moses, "Was it because there were no graves in Egypt that you brought us to the desert to die? What have you done to us by bringing us out of Egypt? [12] Didn't we say to you in Egypt, 'Leave us alone; let us serve the Egyptians'? It would have been better for us to serve the Egyptians than to die in the desert!"

It is what it is…but it is not what it looks like…

Exodus 14:13-16 (NIV) Moses answered the people, "Do not be afraid. *Stand firm and you will see the deliverance the LORD* will bring you today. The Egyptians you see today you will never see again. [14] *The LORD will fight for you; you need only to be still."* [15] Then the LORD said to Moses, "Why are you crying out to me? *Tell the Israelites to move on.* [16] *Raise your staff and stretch out your hand over the sea to divide the water so that the Israelites can go through the sea on dry ground.*

The Issue of Blood
It is what it is…but it's not what it looks like!!!

➢ After she spent all she had

➢ After she had no other place to go
➢ She knew that she too... has to stand

Mark 5:25-34 (NIV) And a woman was there who had been subject to bleeding for twelve years. [26] She had suffered a great deal under the care of many doctors and had spent all she had, yet instead of getting better she grew worse.

It is what it is...but it is not what it looks like...

[27] When she heard about Jesus, she came up behind him in the crowd and touched his cloak, [28] because she thought, *"If I just touch his clothes, I will be healed." * [29] Immediately her bleeding stopped and she felt in her body that she was freed from her suffering. [30] At once Jesus realized that power had gone out from him. He turned around in the crowd and asked, "Who touched my clothes?" [31] "You see the people crowding against you," his disciples answered, "and yet you can ask, 'Who touched me?'" [32] But Jesus kept looking around to see who had done it. [33] Then the woman, knowing what had happened to her, came and fell at his feet and, trembling with fear, told him the whole truth. [34] He said to her, *"Daughter, your faith has healed you. Go in peace and be freed from your suffering."*

Jairus's daughter was dead!!!!
It is what it is…but it is not what it looks like…

Mark 5:22-23 (NIV) Then one of the synagogue rulers, named Jairus, came there. Seeing Jesus, he fell at his feet 23 and pleaded earnestly with him, "My little daughter is dying. Please come and put your hands on her so that she will be healed and live."

Mark 5:38 (NIV) When they came to the home of the synagogue ruler, Jesus saw a commotion, with people crying and wailing loudly.

It is what it is…but it is not what it looks like…

Mark 5:39-42 (NIV) He went in and said to them, "Why all this commotion and wailing? The child is not dead but asleep." **40** But they laughed at him. After he put them all out, he took the child's father and mother and the disciples who were with him, and went in where the child was. **41** He took her by the hand and said to her, "Little girl, I say to you, get up!" **42** *Immediately the girl stood up and walked around…*

3 Hebrews boys were thrown into the fire...
It is what it is...but it is not what it looks like....

Daniel 3:19-27 (NIV) Then Nebuchadnezzar was furious with Shadrach, Meshach and Abednego, and his attitude toward them changed. He ordered the furnace heated seven times hotter than usual [20] and commanded some of the strongest soldiers in his army to tie up Shadrach, Meshach and Abednego and throw them into the blazing furnace. [21] So these men, wearing their robes, trousers, turbans and other clothes, were bound and thrown into the blazing furnace. [22] The king's command was so urgent and the furnace so hot that the flames of the fire killed the soldiers who took up Shadrach, Meshach and Abednego, [23] and these three men, firmly tied, fell into the blazing furnace.

It is what it is...but it is not what it looks like...

[24] Then King Nebuchadnezzar leaped to his feet in amazement and asked his advisers, "Weren't there three men that we tied up and threw into the fire?" They replied, "Certainly, O king." [25] He said, "Look! *I see four men walking around in the fire, unbound and*

unharmed, and the *__fourth looks like a son of__* *__the gods.__* " ²⁶ Nebuchadnezzar then approached the opening of the blazing furnace and shouted, "Shadrach, Meshach and Abednego, servants of the Most High God, come out! Come here!" So Shadrach, Meshach and Abednego came out of the fire, ²⁷ and the satraps, prefects, governors and royal advisers crowded around them. They saw that *the fire had not harmed their bodies, nor was a hair of their heads singed; their robes were not scorched, and there was no smell of fire on them.*

Widow was going to eat her last and die....
It is what it is...but it is not what it looks like....

1 Kings 17:9-16 (NIV) "Go at once to Zarephath of Sidon and stay there. I have commanded a widow in that place to supply you with food." ¹⁰ So he went to Zarephath. When he came to the town gate, a widow was there gathering sticks. He called to her and asked, "Would you bring me a little water in a jar so I may have a drink?" ¹¹ As she was going to get it, he called, "And bring me, please, a piece of bread." ¹² "As surely as the LORD your God lives," she replied, "I don't have any bread--only a handful of flour in a jar and a little oil in a jug. I am gathering a few sticks to take home and make a meal for

myself and my son, that we may eat it--and die."

It is what it is…but it is not what it looks like…

¹⁵ She went away and did as Elijah had told her. So *there was food every day for Elijah and for the woman and her family.* ¹⁶ For <u>the jar of flour was not used up and the jug of oil did not run dry</u>, in keeping with the word of the LORD spoken by Elijah.

Lazarus was dead… It is what it is…but it is not what it looks like….

John 11:1-3 (NIV) Now a man named Lazarus was sick. He was from Bethany, the village of Mary and her sister Martha. ² This Mary, whose brother Lazarus now lay sick, was the same one who poured perfume on the Lord and wiped his feet with her hair. ³ So the sisters sent word to Jesus, "Lord, the one you love is sick."

John 11:14 (NIV) So then Jesus told them plainly, "Lazarus is dead,

John 11:17 (NIV) On his arrival, Jesus found that Lazarus had already been in the tomb for four days.

John 11:21 (NIV) "Lord," Martha said to Jesus, "if you had been here, my brother would not have died.

John 11:32-35 (NIV) When Mary reached the place where Jesus was and saw him, she fell at his feet and said, "Lord, if you had been here, my brother would not have died." [33] When Jesus saw her weeping, and the Jews who had come along with her also weeping, he was deeply moved in spirit and troubled. [34] "Where have you laid him?" he asked. "Come and see, Lord," they replied. [35] Jesus wept.

John 11:38-39 (NIV) Jesus, once more deeply moved, came to the tomb. It was a cave with a stone laid across the entrance. [39] "Take away the stone," he said. "But, Lord," said Martha, the sister of the dead man, "by this time there is a bad odor, for he has been there four days."

It is what it is...but it is not what it looks like...

John 11:43-44 (NIV) Jesus called in a loud voice, "Lazarus, come out!" [44] *The dead man came out, his hands and feet wrapped with strips of linen,* and a cloth around his face. Jesus said to them, *"Take off the grave clothes and let him go."*

Jesus was put on the cross.....

It is what it is…but it is not what it looks like….

Luke 23:44-46 (NIV) It was now about the sixth hour, and darkness came over the whole land until the ninth hour, [45] for the sun stopped shining. And the curtain of the temple was torn in two. [46] Jesus called out with a loud voice, "Father, into your hands I commit my spirit." When he had said this, he breathed his last.

It is what it is…but it is not what it looks like…

Luke 24:1-3 (NIV) On the first day of the week, very early in the morning, the women took the spices they had prepared and went to the tomb. *[2] They found the stone rolled away from the tomb,* [3] but when they entered, *they did not find the body of the Lord Jesus.*

32

Laugh now...or laugh later... BUT

don't let Satan get the last laugh.

Props:
Give everyone a "Laffy Taffy" with the title on it... "Don't Let Satan get the Last LAUGH!"

Balaam was into witchcraft. He used sorcery and manipulation against his enemies.

In verse 5 Balaam was hired by Balak to bring a curse upon his enemies (Israel) so he would defeat them.

> ➤ Balaam somewhere in the midst of these testings, had a relationship with God and began to walk with God.

179

- In Number 22:20, God tells Balaam to go with the men of Balak.
- When he goes...God gets very angry
- Not because he goes, but because God knows his heart and that he is still entertaining Balak's offer.
- In vs. 17- Balak offers him, high position and anything he wants
- Lets see what happens when he refused to do what God tells him to do and when our heart is not where it should be with God:

Numbers 22:21-33 (NIV) Balaam got up in the morning, saddled his donkey and went with the princes of Moab. [22] But God was very angry when he went, and the angel of the LORD stood in the road to oppose him. Balaam was riding on his donkey, and his two servants were with him. [23] When the donkey saw the angel of the LORD standing in the road with a drawn sword in his hand, she turned off the road into a field. Balaam beat her to get her back on the road. [24] Then the angel of the LORD stood in a narrow path between two vineyards, with walls on both sides. [25] When the donkey saw the angel of the LORD, she pressed close to the wall, crushing Balaam's foot against it. So he beat her again. [26] Then the angel of the LORD moved on ahead and stood in a narrow place where there was no room to turn, either to the right or to the left. [27] When the donkey saw the angel of the LORD, she lay down under Balaam, and he was angry and beat

her with his staff. [28] Then the LORD opened the donkey's mouth, and she said to Balaam, "What have I done to you to make you beat me these three times?" [29] Balaam answered the donkey, "You have made a fool of me! If I had a sword in my hand, I would kill you right now." [30] The donkey said to Balaam, "Am I not your own donkey, which you have always ridden, to this day? Have I been in the habit of doing this to you?" "No," he said. [31] Then the LORD opened Balaam's eyes, and he saw the angel of the LORD standing in the road with his sword drawn. So he bowed low and fell facedown. [32] The angel of the LORD asked him, "Why have you beaten your donkey these three times? I have come here to oppose you because your path is a reckless one before me. [33] The donkey saw me and turned away from me these three times. If she had not turned away, I would certainly have killed you by now, but I would have spared her."

➤ In the eyes of these servants of Balak, Balaam thought the donkey was making him look bad.

➤ He answers the donkey and says…. You have embarrassed me…or made me look bad in front of these servants.

➤ Balaam, was so caught up with doing his own thing, even when he knew what God was requiring of him and he was blinded to his sin

- HOW many times can we see everyone's faults, but we can not see our own?
- Balaam was turning aside Gods will for fame and fortune
- But once again, God stopped him in his tracks and God spares his life and speaks to him again
- AREN'T YOU GLAD GOD DIDN'T KILL YOU WHEN HE COULD HAVE AND HE GAVE YOU ANOTHER CHANCE?
- Do you really need to go home and have your DOG tell you what Gods will is… like the donkey had to tell Balaam?

God uses Balaam to talk to Balak
- Balak did not have a relationship with God…
- So God used Balaam, who Balak had faith in
- There was 4 times that God gave a message to Balaam to give to Balak (Oracles)

1ˢᵗ Oracle:

God promises to multiply Israel and bless them.

Balak responds in:

Numbers 23:11-12 (NIV) **Balak said to Balaam,** *"What have you done to me? I brought you to curse my enemies, but you have done nothing but bless them!"* [12] **He**

answered, "Must I not speak what the LORD puts in my mouth?"

2nd *Oracle:*

Balak takes him to a different mountain to send down curses…because apparently the first one back fired…but once again, God blesses Balak's enemy:

Numbers 23:19-20 (NIV) *God is not a man, that he should lie, nor a son of man, that he should change his mind.* Does he speak and then not act? Does he promise and not fulfill? [20] I have received a command to bless; he has blessed, and I cannot change it.

Balak gets infuriated and says:
Numbers 23:25-26 (NIV) Then Balak said to Balaam, *"Neither curse them at all nor bless them at all!"* [26] Balaam answered, "Did I not tell you I must do whatever the LORD says?"

3rd *Oracle:*

Balak takes Balaam to a 3rd location to send curses on Israel.

Numbers 24:1-9 (NIV) Now *when Balaam saw that it pleased the LORD to bless Israel, he did not resort to sorcery as at other times,* but turned his face toward the desert. [2] When Balaam looked out and saw Israel encamped tribe by tribe, the Spirit of God came upon him [3] and he uttered his oracle: "The oracle

of Balaam (son of Beor), the oracle of one whose eye sees clearly, [4] the oracle of one who hears the words of God, who sees a vision from the Almighty, who falls prostrate, and whose eyes are opened: [5] "How beautiful are your tents, O Jacob, your dwelling places, O Israel! [6] *"Like valleys they spread out, like gardens beside a river, like aloes planted by the LORD, like cedars beside the waters. [7] Water will flow from their buckets; their seed will have abundant water.* "Their king will be greater than Agag; their kingdom will be exalted. [8] "God brought them out of Egypt; they have the strength of a wild ox. They devour hostile nations and break their bones in pieces; with their arrows they pierce them. [9] Like a lion they crouch and lie down, like a lioness--who dares to rouse them? *"May those who bless you be blessed and those who curse you be cursed!"*

Balak's response:

Numbers 24:10-11 (NIV) Then Balak's anger burned against Balaam. He struck his hands together and said to him, *"I summoned you to curse my enemies, but you have blessed them these three times.* [11] Now leave at once and go home! I said I would reward you handsomely, *but the LORD has kept you from being rewarded."*

4*th* Oracle

Balaam tells Balak that he will be destroyed by Israel and they each go their separate ways.

184

After a failed business, not being able to put curses on peoples lives and able to use sorcery and magic, he then turns to the Lord and the Lord uses him. But Balaam never got the lust of fame and fortune out of his life and spirit and it would ultimately cost him his life. After betraying God, and realizing his days of sorcery was over because of how Balak's life turned out. Balaam turned to leading people into sin and immorality.

Numbers 25:1-5 (NIV)   While Israel was staying in Shittim, *the men began to indulge in sexual immorality with Moabite women,* [2] who invited them to the sacrifices to their gods. The people ate and bowed down before these gods. [3] So *Israel joined in worshiping the Baal* (of Peor). And the Lord's anger burned against them. [4] The LORD said to Moses, *"Take all the leaders of these people, kill them* and expose them in broad daylight before the LORD, so that the Lord's fierce anger may turn away from Israel." [5] So Moses said to Israel's judges, *"Each of you must put to death those of your men who have joined in worshiping the Baal* (of Peor)."

Numbers 31:8 (NIV)   Among their victims were Evi, Rekem, Zur, Hur and Reba--the five kings of Midian. *They also killed Balaam son of Beor with the sword.*

AND IT WAS REMEMBERED THROUGHOUT THE WORD....

2 Peter 2:15-16 (NIV) They have left the straight way and wandered off to follow *the way of Balaam son of Beor*, who loved the wages of wickedness. [16] But he was rebuked for his wrongdoing by a donkey--a beast without speech--who spoke with a man's voice and restrained the prophet's madness.

Jude 1:10-13 (NIV) Yet these men speak abusively against whatever they do not understand; and what things they do understand by instinct, like unreasoning animals--these are the very things that destroy them. [11] Woe to them! They have taken the way of Cain; they have rushed for profit into *Balaam's error*; they have been destroyed in Korah's rebellion. [12] These men are blemishes at your love feasts, eating with you without the slightest qualm--shepherds who feed only themselves. They are clouds without rain, blown along by the wind; autumn trees, without fruit and uprooted-- twice dead. [13] They are wild waves of the sea, foaming up their shame; wandering stars, for whom blackest darkness has been reserved forever.

DON'T LET SATAN GET THE LAST LAUGH IN YOUR LIFE!!

33

Mistakes found In the Bible

Props:
You will need a book....THAT LOOKS LIKE A BIBLE...that you can tear up and a fake burning Bible. On the screen flashing as you come to the platform...
MISTAKES FOUND IN THE BIBLE!!

Now I know you'll have to pick yourself off of the floor, after screaming, Pastor has done it now! He has just gone to far blaspheming our Bible."

I know that you can't wait for the end of this service so you can get on your telephone or computer to broadcast afar saying, "Have you heard that Pastor is departing from the faith?"

Now, before you call your friends and family and say that you heard that Pastor says that there are mistakes in the Bible, you need to hold your horses until you hear me out! I stated that there **are mistakes found in the Bible!** The mistakes are right before your eyes.

Mistake #1:
Eve Made The Mistake Of Listening To The Devil

Genesis 3:2-6 And the woman said unto the serpent, We may eat of the fruit of the trees of the garden: ³ But of the fruit of the tree which is in the midst of the garden, God hath said, Ye shall not eat of it, neither shall ye touch it, lest ye die. ⁴ And the serpent said unto the woman, Ye shall not surely die: ⁵ For God doth know that in the day ye eat thereof, then your eyes shall be opened, and ye shall be as gods, knowing good and evil. ⁶ And when the woman saw that the tree was good for food, and that it was pleasant to the eyes, and a tree to be desired to make one wise, she took of the fruit thereof, and did eat, and gave also unto her husband with her; and he did eat.

➤ Eve made a terrible mistake
➤ She listened to the Devil…

How many time have you made that SAME MISTAKE???

Mistake #2:

Abraham Made The Mistake Of Taking Lot With Him

Genesis 12:1-5 Now the LORD had said unto Abram, Get thee out of thy country, _and from thy kindred,_ and from thy father's house, unto a land that I will shew thee: [2] And I will make of thee a great nation, and I will bless thee, and make thy name great; and thou shalt be a blessing: [3] And I will bless them that bless thee, and curse him that curseth thee: and in thee shall all families of the earth be blessed. [4] So Abram departed, as the LORD had spoken unto him; and Lot went with him: and Abram was seventy and five years old when he departed out of Haran. [5] And Abram took Sarai his wife, and Lot his brother's son, and all their substance that they had gathered, and the souls that they had gotten in Haran; and they went forth to go into the land of Canaan; and into the land of Canaan they came.

- ➢ GOD said, "Don't carry your family."
- ➢ Lot and Abrams herdsmen fell out… and
- ➢ Abram and Lot had to part ways…
- ➢ Abram offered Lot the hills or the valleys…
- ➢ Lot took the best and went for the valley…
- ➢ Lot ended up in Sodom.
- ➢ And…well…you know the rest of the story..
- ➢ Sometimes…God has to get you away from some of your relatives…
- ➢ It is a mistake…when you stay around them….AMEN??

Mistake #3: Moses Made The Mistake Of Smiting The Rock

Numbers 20:7-13 And the LORD spake unto Moses, saying, [8] Take the rod, and gather thou the assembly together, thou, and Aaron thy brother, and _speak ye unto the rock_ before their eyes; and it shall give forth his water, and thou shalt bring forth to them water out of the rock: so thou shalt give the congregation and their beasts drink. [9] And Moses took the rod from before the LORD, as he commanded him. [10] And Moses and Aaron gathered the congregation together before the rock, and he said unto them, Hear now, ye rebels; must we fetch you water out of this rock? [11] And Moses lifted up his hand, and _with his rod he smote the rock twice:_ and the water came out abundantly, and the congregation drank, and their beasts also. [12] And the LORD spake unto Moses and Aaron, Because ye believed me not, to sanctify me in the eyes of the children of Israel, _therefore ye shall not bring this congregation into the land which I have given them._ [13] This is the water of Meribah; because the children of Israel strove with the LORD, and he was sanctified in them.

- ➤ Moses missed the promised land…because of his mistake
- ➤ We must ask ourselves, before we fall short… is it worth it

➤ In raising our children…they watch us…is it worth what they see
➤ Or…what they hear us say…or what they see us do????

This mistake cost Moses dearly. He was denied the opportunity to go into the Promised Land.

Mistake #4: Samson Made the Mistake by giving in to Delilah

Judges 16:19-21 And she made him sleep upon her knees; and she called for a man, and she caused him to shave off the seven locks of his head; and she began to afflict him, and his strength went from him. [20] And she said, The Philistines be upon thee, Samson. And he awoke out of his sleep, and said, I will go out as at other times before, and shake myself. And he wist not that the LORD was departed from him. [21] But the Philistines took him, and put out his eyes, and brought him down to Gaza, and bound him with fetters of brass; and he did grind in the prison house.

➤ Samson's mistake…cost him his life…
➤ Not only his life…but all that was in the coliseum

> We instruct our children when driving…because one moment of neglect…can cost them their life…

One time sleeping with the wrong person…and it can cost you your life.

Samson laid his head in the devils lap. Oh, what a mistake!

Mistake #5:
The Jews Made The Mistake Of Not Recognizing Their Messiah

John 1:11-12 He came unto his own, and his own received him not. [12] But as many as received him, to them gave he power to become the sons of God, even to them that believe on his name:

> The Jews made the mistake of not recognizing Jesus as the Messiah…
> But those that did… was given POWER…to become the sons of God.
> Praise God… I have made the mistake of not accepting him…
> But know that my eyes have been open… I never want to deny Him!!
> Don't make that mistake of denying Him and then going into an eternity!
> Hell is really and for a VERY LONG TIME.

Mistake #6:
The Devil Made The Mistake Of Thinking That He Could Hold Jesus In The Grave

Luke 24:1-7 Now upon the first day of the week, very early in the morning, they came unto the sepulchre, bringing the spices which they had prepared, and certain others with them. ² And they found the stone rolled away from the sepulchre. ³ And they entered in, and found not the body of the Lord Jesus. ⁴ And it came to pass, as they were much perplexed thereabout, behold, two men stood by them in shining garments: ⁵ And as they were afraid, and bowed down their faces to the earth, they said unto them, Why seek ye the living among the dead? ⁶ He is not here, but is risen: remember how he spake unto you when he was yet in Galilee, ⁷ Saying, The Son of man must be delivered into the hands of sinful men, and be crucified, and _the third day rise again._

- ➢ The enemy made a huge mistake… by thinking he could destroy our savior.
- ➢ He only helped to perfect the plan of salvation…
- ➢ Unless Jesus died… I could not live
- ➢ Unless He bleed, I couldn't be healed
- ➢ Unless He be beaten… I could not be delivered…

➤ BUT praise God…He paid the
price…therefore I LIVE with Him!!!

Mistake #7:
YOU Made The Mistake Of Judging Me Before You Heard Me Out.

Now, do you understand why I say that there are mistakes in the Bible? Notice that I didn't say **WITH** the Bible, I said "IN" the Bible. The fact is, there is nothing wrong with the Bible…the problem lies within us. It's perfect, and man is very much mistaken when he tries to tamper with it!

Hebrew 4:12 (KJV) For the word of God is quick, and powerful, and sharper than any two edged sword, piercing even to the dividing asunder of soul and spirit, and of the joints and marrow, and is a discerner of the thoughts and intents of the heart.

Jeremiah 20:9 (KJV) Then I said, I will not make mention of him, nor speak any more in his name. But his word was in mine heart as a burning fire shut up in my bones, and I was weary with forbearing, and I could not stay.

34

Nothing worth going back for!!!

PROPS:
You will need a:
Plow- Prop #1 – Covered with a sheet at the left of the platform
Pillar of Salt- Prop #2 – Covered with a sheet- Center stage
A finish line- Prop #3 Clearly marked at the right side of stage
A HUGE Trophy – Prop #4 Covered with a sheet

Luke 9:62 (NIV) Jesus replied, *"No one who puts his hand to the plow and looks back is fit for service in the kingdom of God."*

Genesis 19:15-26 (NIV) With the coming of dawn, the angels urged Lot, saying, "Hurry! Take your wife and your two daughters who are here, or you will be swept away when the city is punished." [16] When he hesitated, the men grasped his hand and the hands of his wife and of his two daughters and led them safely out of the city, for the LORD was merciful to them. [17] As soon as they had brought them out, one of them said, "Flee for your lives! Don't look back, and don't stop anywhere in the plain! Flee to the mountains or you will be swept away!" [18] But Lot said to them, "No, my lords, please! [19] Your servant has found favor in your eyes, and you have shown great kindness to me in sparing my life. But I can't flee to the mountains; this disaster will overtake me, and I'll die. [20] Look, here is a town near enough to run to, and it is small. Let me flee to it--it is very small, isn't it? Then my life will be spared." [21] He said to him, "Very well, I will grant this request too; I will not overthrow the town you speak of. [22] But flee there quickly, because I cannot do anything until you reach it." (That is why the town was called Zoar.) [23] By the time Lot reached Zoar, the sun had risen over the land. [24] Then the LORD rained down burning sulfur on Sodom and Gomorrah--from the LORD out of the heavens. [25] Thus he overthrew those cities and the entire plain, including all those living in the cities--and also the vegetation in the land. [26] *But Lot's wife looked back, and she became a pillar of salt.*

Luke 17:24-33 (NIV) For the Son of Man in his day will be like the lightning, which flashes and lights up the sky from one end to the other. [25] But first he must suffer many things and be rejected by this generation. [26] "Just as it was in the days of Noah, so also will it be in the days of the Son of Man. [27] People were eating, drinking, marrying and being given in marriage up to *the day Noah* entered the ark. Then the flood came and destroyed them all. [28] "It was the same in the *days of Lot.* People were eating and drinking, buying and selling, planting and building. [29] But the day Lot left Sodom, fire and sulfur rained down from heaven and destroyed them all. [30] "It will be just like this on the day the Son of Man is revealed. [31] On that day no one who is on the roof of his house, with his goods inside, should go down to get them. Likewise, no one in the field should go back for anything. [32] *Remember Lot's wife!* [33] *Whoever tries to keep his life will lose it, and whoever loses his life will preserve it.*

Romans 8:13-14 (NIV)   ... *if you live according to the sinful nature,*(IF YOU LOOK BACK) *you will die;* but *if by the Spirit* (IF YOU LOOK FORWARD) you put to death the misdeeds of the body, *you will live,* [14] because those who are led by the Spirit of God are sons of God.

WHAT IS BEHIND YOU???

Matthew 16:23 (NIV) Jesus turned and said to Peter, *"Get behind me, Satan!* You are *a stumbling block* to me; you do not have in mind the things of God, but the things of men."

A. Satan

B. A stumbling block

Looking behind you … will lead you into hell!!!

Mark 9:42-48 (NIV) "And if anyone causes one of these little ones who believe in me to sin, it would be better for him to be thrown into the sea with a large millstone tied around his neck. [43] If your hand causes you to sin, cut it off. It is better for you to enter life maimed than with two hands to go into hell, where the fire never goes out. [44][45] And if your foot causes you to sin, cut it off. It is better for you to enter life crippled than to have two feet and be thrown into hell. [46][47] And if your eye causes you to sin, pluck it out. It is better for you to enter the kingdom of God with one eye than to have two eyes and be thrown into hell, [48] where "'their worm does not die, and the fire is not quenched.'

WHAT IS AHEAD OF YOU???

Philippians 3:13-14 (NIV) Brothers, I do not consider myself yet to have taken hold of it. But one thing I do: Forgetting what is behind and straining toward what is ahead, [14] _I press on toward the goal to win the prize_ for which God has called me heavenward in Christ Jesus.

Isaiah 43:18-19 (NIV) "Forget the former things; do not dwell on the past. [19] See, _I am_

198

doing a new thing! Now it springs up; do you not perceive it? I am making *a way in the desert and streams in the wasteland.*

➤ A new thing… places you have never been, people you have never seen, blessings never imagined.
➤ A path in the desert
➤ Steams in your dry places…

1 Corinthians 2:9-10 (NIV) However, as it is written: "No eye has seen, no ear has heard, *no mind has conceived what God has prepared for those who love him"--* [10] but God has revealed it to us by his Spirit. The Spirit searches all things, even the deep things of God.

John 14:1-4 (NIV) "Do not let your hearts be troubled. Trust in God ; trust also in me. [2] *In my Father's house are many rooms;* if it were not so, I would have told you. I am going there to prepare a place for you. [3] And if *I go and prepare a place for you,* I will come back and take you to be with me that you also may be where I am. [4] You know the way to the place where I am going."

35

Picked out to be Picked On

Props:
You will need:
REAL GEEK with: Glasses with tape; High pants; Billy-bob teeth and bow tie

Have you ever noticed...that you don't have to tell the kids who the class geek is? They automatically know!!! It is not something they have to be taught.
I have never seen anyone teach their child how to lie...but they ALL know how to do it...and if I may add...at a very YOUNG age.

- ➤ I believe that sometimes... we were picked out... to be picked on...
- ➤ How many of you were picked on as a kid????

Illustration: SHOW SLIDES of some congregation member's high school pictures.

Job was PICKED OUT...TO BE PICKED ON!!!

Job 1:6-8 (NIV) One day the angels came to present themselves before the LORD, and Satan also came with them. ⁷ The LORD said to Satan, "Where have you come from?" Satan answered the LORD, _"From roaming through the earth and going back and forth in it."_ ⁸ Then the LORD said to Satan, _"Have you considered my servant Job? There is no one on earth like him; he is blameless and upright, a man who fears God and shuns evil."_

➢ Job was truly picked out to be picked on
➢ Satan joined in on the angels party
➢ God RECOMMENDED Job to be picked out…and to be picked on.
➢ How many of you all ever feel that way?
➢ WELL, Job remained faithful unto the end…
➢ He lost it all
➢ Family, friends, finance, children, his health…everything!!!
➢ But he hung on…
➢ We know what the BIBLE says in Job 42, that Job got back twice as much in return…
➢ DOUBLE FOR HIS TROUBLE…
➢ HOW MANY OF YOU ARE ASKING BACK DOUBLE…EVERYTHING THE ENEMY HAS TAKEN…
➢ Twice the peace
➢ Twice the marriage
➢ Twice the Finances

➤ Twice the Future…

John 15:16 (NIV) You did not choose me, but I chose you and appointed you to go and bear fruit--fruit that will last. Then the Father will give you whatever you ask in my name.

JESUS WAS PICKED OUT…TO BE PICKED ON…
  ➤ Just like Job in the OT
  ➤ JESUS in the NT was picked out by God to be picked on…
  ➤ Remember… when God volunteers you to be picked on….
  ➤ GOD IS ABOUT TO BLESS YOU
  ➤ HE IS JUST SETTING YOU UP!!!

Matthew 3:16-17 (NIV) _As soon_ as Jesus was baptized, he went up out of the water. At that moment _heaven was opened, and he saw the Spirit of God descending like a dove and lighting on him._ [17] And _a voice from heaven said, "This is my Son, whom I love; with him I am well pleased."_

Matthew 4:1-11 (NIV) Then _Jesus was led by the Spirit_ into the _desert_ to be tempted by the devil. [2] After fasting forty days and forty nights, he was hungry. [3] The tempter came to him and said, _"If you are the Son of God, tell these stones to become bread."_ [4] Jesus answered, "It is written: 'Man does not live on bread alone, but on every word that comes from the mouth of God.'" [5] Then the

devil took him to the holy city and had him stand on the highest point of the temple. [6] **_"If you are the Son of God," he said, "throw yourself down. For it is written: "'He will command his angels concerning you, and they will lift you up in their hands, so that you will not strike your foot against a stone.'"_** [7] Jesus answered him, "It is also written: 'Do not put the Lord your God to the test.'" [8] Again, the devil took him to a very high mountain and showed him all the kingdoms of the world and their splendor. [9] **_"All this I will give you," he said, "if you will bow down and worship me."_** [10] Jesus said to him, "Away from me, Satan! For it is written: 'Worship the Lord your God, and serve him only.'" [11] **_Then the devil left him, and angels came and attended him._**

➤ Jesus was picked out to be picked on…
➤ Again…see the comparison…
➤ Job was recommended by God to Satan
➤ Job was given Double for his Trouble
➤ Then… God had Satan to lead Jesus into the wilderness…
➤ God sends his Angels to comfort Him…
➤ They both were in better place and positions for what they had to go through.

THEY WERE PICKED OUT TO BE PICKED ON….

AS YOU SEE...BOTH OF THESE...JOB AND JESUS...DID THE RIGHT THING AND RECEIVED THE RIGHT REWARD...

- ➢ You have to stick it out
- ➢ You have to know that God is in control
- ➢ You have to know that He has your best interest in mind.
- ➢ You have to know that He is not going to let you sink...
- ➢ He didn't teach you how to swim....to let you drown.

Romans 8:28-31 (NIV) And _we know that in all things God works for the good of those who love him, who have been called according to his purpose._ ²⁹ For those God foreknew he also predestined to be conformed to the likeness of his Son, that he might be the firstborn among many brothers. ³⁰ And _those he predestined, he also called; those he called, he also justified; those he justified, he also glorified_. ³¹ What, then, shall we say in response to this? _If God is for us, who can be against us?_

- ➢ I am destined to be blessed
- ➢ I am destined to be the head...and not the tail
- ➢ I am destined to be the lender and not the borrower...
- ➢ Anyone here destined...to be BLESSED???

Romans 8:37 (NIV) ...we are more than conquerors through him who loved us.

36

PRINGLES... GOD'S POTATO CHIP!!!

PROPS:
You will need Large bags of: Lays, Doritos, Cheetos, Fritos, Ruffles, Cracker Jacks(BOX), a regular size can of Pringles, 10 stacker cans of small Pringle and a twin pack of Pringles

DO NOT PUT TITLE ON THE SCREEN UNTIL YOU FINISH INTRODUCTION AND GIVE IT OUT.

1 Corinthians 14:30-40 (KJV) If any thing be revealed to another that sitteth by, let the first hold his peace. [31] For ye may all prophesy one by one, that all may learn, and all may be comforted. [32] And the spirits of the prophets are subject to the prophets. [33] For God is not the author of confusion, but of peace, as in all churches of the saints. [34] Let your women keep silence in the churches: for it is not permitted unto them to speak;

but they are commanded to be under obedience, as also saith the law. [35] **And if they will learn any thing, let them ask their husbands at home: for it is a shame for women to speak in the church.** [36] **What? came the word of God out from you? or came it unto you only?** [37] **If any man think himself to be a prophet, or spiritual, let him acknowledge that the things that I write unto you are the commandments of the Lord.** [38] **But if any man be ignorant, let him be ignorant.** [39] **Wherefore, brethren, covet to prophesy, and forbid not to speak with tongues.** [40] _**Let all things be done decently and in order.**_

I am always trying to find everyday items to allow God to speak to me and give me a revelation and a fresh word.

Today I want to show you how a can of "PRINGLES" can teach you a principle to keep you from being stressed or even having a nervous break down.

This morning... It happens to be PRINGLES Potato Chips

HOW MANY OF YOU LIKE CHIPS???

You may remember some of these famous slogans from Potato Chip commercials. If so it may just tell your age.

Lay's Potato Chips---You cant eat just one….
Doritos---Nacho Cheesier Chips
Cheetos---The Cheese that goes CRUNCH
Frito's- Had the Frito Bandito --- Ayiee, yie-yie-yieeee,
I am dee Frito Bandito.
I love Frito's Corn Chips,
I love dem I do.
I love Frito's Corn Chips,
I take dem from you.
Ruffles- Have Ridges…. You must roll your tongue
Cracker Jacks---A prize in every Box

I asked Bro._____ what his favorite chip was this week and he said "POKER"

PRINGLES SLOGAN: Once you pop'em… you just can't stop'em.

Let's try it this morning and see if you can hear them pop when I open them… (Have drummer to do a pop sound on the drums when you open the can)

(Take all the chips out…showing their shape and how they are organized and stacked in the can)

The first thing that you will notice is that they are stacked in the can…. THEY ARE ORGANIZED!!!!!
GOD IS ALSO VERY ORGANIZED!!!!!

- Even God had a plan….and followed it!!!
- In Genesis….creation was ORGANIZED by God!!!
- He didn't just get up one day and say …hmmmm…what am I going to do today…. God had a plan
- NOTICE that God even planned HIS REST!!!
- On the 7th Day….He rested.
- The Bible Is GODS schedule book.
- It is his Organized plan of what He is doing and Going to do
- NO one can say…they didn't know he was coming back…HE SAID IT.

John 14:1-4 (KJV) Let not your heart be troubled: ye believe in God, believe also in me. ² In my Father's house are many mansions: if it were not so, I would have told you. I go to prepare a place for you. ³ And if I go and prepare a place for you, I will come again, and receive you unto myself; that where I am, there ye may be also. ⁴ And whither I go ye know, and the way ye know.

He really is coming back…He has already planned for it!!!

Open a Bag of regular potato chips--- pour them into a bowl

...."These chips are a mess....just like most of our lives.

> We have NO order in our life
> We come in this morning in a mess....a HOT MESS!!!
> Scripture says... let all things be done decently and in order

At the bottom of the bag are crumbs.... "Can I ever get my life back together???

Get a volunteer to come up... have them to try to stack the chips ...the Pringles first....then from the regular bag....

> YOU NEED TO GET YOU LIFE STRAIGHTENED OUT...
> YOU NEED YOU LIFE TO BE IN ORDER!!!!
> GET YOUR LIFE TOGETHER THE WAY GOD PLANNED IT!!
> DECENTLY AND IN ORDER!!!
> THE FIRST THING WE MUST DO...IS GET THINGS IN ORDER WITH GOD.

EXAMPLE OF THE JUDGE:
> A Judge will call: "ORDER IN THE COURT"
> It is time that we call order back!!!!
> ORDER IN THE CHURCH
> ORDER IN THE HOME

- ➤ ORDER IN MY LIFE
- ➤ ORDER IN MY MARRIAGE
- ➤ When a child tells the parent what to do...your life is OUT OF ORDER!!!!
- ➤ When you have to go to the rest room… and you are about to burst…and you get to the door and see "OUT OF ORDER" how does it make you feel???

When you look at the BIG bag of chips… it is a mess… it seems overwhelming…what do I do????

You must
1. Organize in little units (Bring out the little cans of Pringles)
   - ➤ How …when I didn't
   - ➤ Marry according to the Bible
   - ➤ Live according to the Bible
   - ➤ Did act the way the Bible teaches

Life is filled with many little compartments of our life!!!
Snack Pack
Regular Can
Twin Can Pringles

LET ME GIVE YOU HOPE…. YOU STACK ENOUGH…LITTLE UNITS UP IN YOUR LIFE…YOU WILL FIND ORDER IN YOUR LIFE!!!

MANY OF YOU ARE HERE TODAY BECAUSE YOU LIFE IS OUR OF CONTROL AND OUT OF ORDER!!!

- ➤ Get your life back today!!!!!
- ➤ Get your:
- ➤ Bible Reading in order
- ➤ Attendance in church in order
- ➤ Christianity in order
- ➤ Finances in order
- ➤ Prayer life in order
- ➤ Marriage in order
- ➤ START SOMEWHERE...START STACKING THIS MORNING.

I CORINTHIANS 14:40 Let all things be done...decently and in order!!!

YOU NEED YOUR LIFE IN ORDER... BY
1. Your church attendance
   a. Your life is out of order when you lay out...

2. Being ON TIME!!!!
   a. It is a sign that you life is out of order...when you cant get anywhere on time!!!!
   b. Departure time... is very important to arrival time!!!
   c. Our problem is.... We get up on Sunday... and try to decide... if we are

going to church!!!! THAT IS NOT ORDER

    d. Order is...tomorrow...we go to church...It is a plan set that will be followed through

    e. ORDER IS KNOWING WHERE YOU WILL BE ON SUNDY MORNING...SUNDAY NIGHT... WEDNESDAY NIGHT!!!

3) Reading your Bible
    a. EVERY day ... that is scriptural...
    b. Get a place
    c. Get a time
    d. Get a Bible...
    e. And DO IT!!!
    f. ORDER is...after you read it...do it!!!

WHEN I HEAR PEOPLE SAY:

➤ Life isn't worth living...
➤ What is the use of going on
➤ Know one understands
➤ What do I have to look forward to...
➤ IT TELLS ME ...THEIR LIFE IS OUT OF ORDER!!!
➤ YOU HAVE TO GET ORGANIZED!!!

4) You Have to PRAY
    a. NOT just over your food
    b. Do you have a place

c. Do you have a time

d. NO WONDER YOUR LIFE IS A MESS!!!

5) Are you WINNING SOULS…
   a. It is our COMMISSION
   b. It is your job and my job

4 step plan:
a. Everyone was born into sin
b. There is a penalty for sin…heaven or hell
c. Jesus paid the price for our sins
d. Now wont you receive him…so your sins will be gone!!!

SUNDAY SCHOOL TEACHERS!!!
Organize your class
Organize your study
Organize your walls…your room… your lesson

Do you know that it took a lot of organizing to have this service:
   ➤ Someone to set the temp and turn on the lights
   ➤ Someone to run sound
   ➤ Someone to run the screen
   ➤ Someone to lead the music
   ➤ Someone to play the music
   ➤ Someone to sing
   ➤ Someone to preach
   ➤ Someone to teach

- ➢ Someone to usher
- ➢ Someone to park
- ➢ Someone to lead the choir
- ➢ Someone to take the offering
- ➢ Someone to work the altars….
- ➢ IT WAS PLANNED AND ORGANIZED!!!! IT HAS ORDER

6) Your FINANCES
   a. It is amazing how many 'Christians" are in financial turmoil
   b. Maybe it is because your finances aren't organized
      1. God gets the first fruit… 10%
      2. Pay bills with the second fruit
      3. Save with the 3rd fruit
      4. and have fun and enjoy the 4th fruit
      5. This is God's ORDER!!!

Today… we have FUN first… pay bills with what is left and leave God totally out!!!!! GET YOUR LIFE IN ORDER!!!

What we often say is this… "My Big screen is more important than giving to GOD!!! Friend … YOU ARE MESSED UP!!!!
ONCE YOU POP'EM … YOU JUST CAN'T STOP'EM.

DON'T LET THE DEVIL TRICK YOU....GET
IT TOGETHER
GET YOU LIFE IN ORDER!!!

37

ROLEX ... QUALITY TAKES TIME

Props:
You need a ROLEX and a TIMEX

If you had a choice of a TIMEX or a ROLEX, which would you take?

Most of us...if not ALL of us would take the ROLEX!! Right?

Why? Because you can buy a real nice Timex for under $50. You can buy them at Wal-Mart, K-Mart, Kohls, or even at CVS. They are available everywhere.

But a ROLEX...You can only find at the most Elite stores. They can run well over $100,000. Even though the do the same thing... the Rolex glides instead of ticks... The Rolex is make of 18 KT gold instead of gold colored metal, the ROLEX has real diamonds instead CZ's...

A Rolex, is much harder to find… and much more expensive… made with only the finest parts… which are made … one at a time… and not on a conveyor belt.

TIMEX MOTTO…. TAKES A LICKING AND KEEPS ON TICKING…

BUT ROLEX MOTTO IS… QUALITY…TAKES TIME!!!

TIMEX PRODUCES…A GREAT
PRODUCT…BUT ALSO PRODUCE
QUANTITY
ROLEX PRODUCES… A BETTER
PRODUCT… AND PRODUCES QUALITY

➢ If you asked your spouse…which they would rather have…quality or quantity… they would most likely pick quality…
➢ What good is it if you spend an entire day together…but sit in front of the TV all day…
➢ They would rather have a nice dinner with your undivided attention away from TV, Radios, Cell phones and palm pilots for one hour than a whole day…which has no substance.

TONIGHT… I WANT YOU TO REALIZE …THAT QUALITY…TAKES TIME!!!!

Genesis 29:16-30 (NIV) Now Laban had two daughters; the name of the older was Leah, and the name of the younger was Rachel. [17] Leah had weak eyes, but Rachel was lovely in form, and beautiful. [18] Jacob was in love with Rachel and said, *"I'll work for you seven years in return for your younger daughter Rachel."* [19] Laban said, "It's better that I give her to you than to some other man. Stay here with me." [20] So Jacob served seven years to get Rachel, but they seemed like only a few days to him because of his love for her. [21] Then Jacob said to Laban, "Give me my wife. My time is completed, and I want to lie with her." [22] So Laban brought together all the people of the place and gave a feast. [23] But when evening came, he took his daughter Leah and gave her to Jacob, and Jacob lay with her. [24] And Laban gave his servant girl Zilpah to his daughter as her maidservant. [25] When morning came, there was Leah! So Jacob said to Laban, "What is this you have done to me? I served you for Rachel, didn't I? Why have you deceived me?" [26] Laban replied, "It is not our custom here to give the younger daughter in marriage before the older one. [27] Finish this daughter's bridal week; then *we will give you the younger one also, in return for another seven years of work."* [28] And Jacob did so. He finished the week with Leah, and then Laban gave him his daughter Rachel to be his wife. [29] Laban gave his servant girl Bilhah to his daughter Rachel as her maidservant. [30] Jacob lay with Rachel also, and he loved Rachel more than

Leah. And *he worked for Laban another seven years.*

> Jacob loved Rachel
> In fact…he loved her so much…that he worked 14 years instead of seven for her.
> He was willing to do 7… but he found out…that quality took time… therefore he was willing to invest another 7 years.
> People jump in and out of marriages… can I tell you
> That QUALITY TAKES TIME!!!
> I fell out of love… How do you fall in and out of love so easily and quickly?
> QUALITY TAKES TIME!!!
> I thought I loved my wife when I married her 21 years ago… Now I know…
> I LOVE MY WIFE…. QUALITY TAKES TIME!!!

John 5:1-9 (NIV) Some time later, Jesus went up to Jerusalem for a feast of the Jews. 2 Now there is in Jerusalem near the Sheep Gate a pool, which in Aramaic is called Bethesda and which is surrounded by five covered colonnades. 3 Here a great number of disabled people used to lie--the blind, the lame, the paralyzed. 4 5 One who was there had been an invalid for thirty-eight years. 6 When Jesus saw him lying there and learned that he had been in this condition for a long time, he asked him, "Do you want to get well?" 7 "Sir," the invalid replied, "I have no

one to help me into the pool when the water is stirred. While I am trying to get in, someone else goes down ahead of me." [8] **Then Jesus said to him, "Get up! Pick up your mat and walk."** [9] **At once the man was cured; he picked up his mat and walked....**

➤ We all know the story of the woman with the issue of blood.
➤ For 12 years she walked around in defeat...
➤ BUT QUALITY TAKES TIME....
➤ WHEN SHE WAS HEALED...SHE WAS HEALED!!

➤ How about the woman that was going to eat her last loaf of bread with her son and die...
➤ She had promised God that she would feed the prophet...
➤ Yet all she had was enough for her and her son...
➤ But she did it any way... and look what happened
➤ HER MEAL BARREL NEVER WENT DRY...
➤ QUALITY TAKES TIME!!!

➤ Remember NAAMAN
➤ He had to leave his town where clean water lay
➤ Had to travel a far distance to dip in muddy water...
➤ Then had to dip not once...but 7 times...

- BUT HE WAS HEALED
- QUALITY TAKES TIME

- How about NOAH
- He had to build a big boat…when it had never rained
- People laughed at him
- It took him 100 years…
- BUT QUALITY TAKES TIME!!!

- Remember Abram and Sarai…
- They wanted a child…
- They went around the promise…and had a maidservant to give them a child
- But that wasn't Gods promise….
- QUALITY TAKES TIME
- At the age of 90 and 100…they had the RIGHT child…
- QUALITY TAKES TIME

38

SITTING IN THE WINDOW SEAL

> **Props:**
> Have a window that can open-Big enough for someone to sit in it.

Acts 20:7-9 (NIV) On the first day of the week we came together to break bread. Paul spoke to the people and, because he intended to leave the next day, kept on talking until midnight. [8] There were many lamps in the upstairs room where we were meeting. [9] Seated in a window was a young man named Eutychus, who was sinking into a deep sleep as Paul talked on and on. When he was sound asleep, he fell to the ground from the third story and was picked up dead.

- ➤ Obviously the people were hungry
- ➤ They came to hear Paul preach
- ➤ They came to stay as long as they had to
- ➤ They filled the room with standing room only

- ➤ There was a young man who came that was in a dangerous position in life.

Eutychus means FORTUNE

Sitting in the window seal

- ➤ You have the option of falling 2 ways...
- ➤ Into the WORLD...or...into the CHURCH
- ➤ FATAL position is BETWEEN the WORD and the WORLD

FACTS:
- ➤ He was 3 stories up
- ➤ Paul had preached a LONG time
- ➤ It was now past midnight
- ➤ The young man fell asleep

THE WINDOW REPRESENTS:

- ➤ The WORLD on one side...The WORD on the other.
- ➤ HOLINESS on one side...UNHOLY on the other.
- ➤ LIGHT and DARKNESS

The BIBLE says that you are either FOR Him or AGAINST Him.

- ➤ Eutychus wants to be in the church
- ➤ YET he wanted to be in the world

- A DANGEROUS PLACE TO BE....
- IN THE WINDOW SEAL.
- We come and we want to feel Gods presence...
- YET ... we want to feel the high of the joint

Eutychus decides to live between the 2 worlds....
- Sunday we want to come to church ...
- Tuesday...having someone come up out of your house.

EUTYCHUS fell asleep
- YOU EVER NOTICE:
- When the choir is singing...everyone likes to shout....
- BUT when the word comes forth.....
- We start Yawning
- Get Sleeping
- Gotta Pee
- Get Thirsty....

IT is a dangerous place to be... to be in God's house for the word and
- Have to go get a drink of water when your word comes
- Have to sleep through your promise
- Have distractions around you when your power is revealed to set you free.

NOTICE:

EUTYCUS...DIDN'T FALL IN THE CHURCH...HE FELL OUT OF THE CHURCH.

- ➤ If he had fallen in the church...he would have been a shorter fall.
- ➤ BUT he fall in the world...3 stories down....
- ➤ The world pronounced him dead.....
- ➤ BUT the church embraced him....

Acts 20:9-12 (NIV)...When he was sound asleep, he fell to the ground from the third story and was picked up dead. [10] Paul went down, threw himself on the young man and put his arms around him. "Don't be alarmed," he said. "He's alive!" [11] Then he went upstairs again and broke bread and ate. After talking until daylight, he left. [12] The people took the young man home alive and were greatly comforted.

- ➤ As a church...
- ➤ We cant push people down or away....
- ➤ We have to lift them up to the throne of grace
- ➤ We have to let them know that we will pick them up from their fall
- ➤ Not talking about them... accusing them....

WE ALL HAVE A PAST!!!!

- ➤ Done things that we are not proud of
- ➤ Been places we wish we had not been
- ➤ Seen things we wish we had not seen
- ➤ Said things we wish we had not said

39

Some Things That Jesus Will Not Do... Until We Do

PROPS:
A bag full of pennies from the bank...$100; a cup, a spoon and a shovel. Everyone needs to be given an envelope when they come in...they will all contain a piece of blank paper, except three which will contain a piece of paper that say, SPOON on one, one will say CUP and the other will say SHOVEL.

The Bible teaches that God has all power and he is able to do all things. But, we can limit Him by not following His Instructions!

Here are just a few things that God says you have to do before He will.

(1) God will not forgive us until we forgive others

Matthew 6:14-15 (KJV) For _if_ ye forgive men their trespasses, _your heavenly Father will also forgive you:_ But i_f_ ye forgive not men their trespasses, _neither will your Father forgive your_ trespasses.

Ephesians 4:23 (KJV) And be ye kind one to another, tenderhearted, _forgiving one another,_ even has Christ hath forgiven you.

Forgive----To give up resentment or the desire to punish.

- ➢ Stop being angry with that one that hurt you…

- ➢ It will only bring you down

- ➢ Don't lower your level…but act and look like Christ…

Matthew 18:18-22 (KJV) Verily I say unto you, Whatsoever ye shall bind on earth shall be bound in heaven: and whatsoever ye shall loose on earth shall be loosed in heaven. [19] Again I say unto you, That if two of you shall agree on earth as touching any thing that they shall ask, it shall be done for them of my Father which is in heaven. [20] For where two or three are gathered together in my name, there am I in the midst of them. [21] Then came Peter to him, and said, Lord, how

oft shall my brother sin against me, and I forgive him? till seven times? [22] Jesus saith unto him, *I say not unto thee, Until seven times: but, Until seventy times seven.*

➢ God wants us to have TRUE FORGIVENESS...
➢ NOT just lip service...
➢ Do you have aught against anyone???

(2) Jesus will not confess you before His Father until we confess Him before men.

Matthew 10:32-33 (KJV) *Whosoever therefore shall confess me before men, him will I confess also before my Father* which is in heaven. But *whosoever shall deny me before men, him will I also deny before my Father* which is in heaven.

A.   This confession is of a person (God Says "You MUST confess me!")

B.   This confession must be public (before men)

C.   This confession results in a promise (I will confess you before My Father in Heaven)

This proves beyond any doubt that a person must be saved **and** confessing that he is saved to this world.

- ➤ Be careful when we become so "HOLY" that 40we don't confess our Savior.

- ➤ OR that we don't witness for Him or

- ➤ Tell others of His goodness....

- ➤ The Bible says... God also has the power to be ashamed of us...if we are ashamed of HIM.

Mark 8:38 (KJV) Whosoever therefore shall be ashamed of me and of my words in this adulterous and sinful generation; of him also shall the Son of man be ashamed, when he cometh in the glory of his Father with the holy angels.

(3) Jesus will not give unto you, until we give unto Him.

Luke 6:38 (KJV) _Give, and it shall be given unto you;_ good measure, pressed down, and shaken together, and running over, shall men give into your bosom. For _with the same measure that ye mete withal it shall be measured to you again._

- ➤ You give respect. You get respect!

- ➤ You give love. You get love!

- ➤ You give money. You get money! This could be the answer as to why you're always broke.

- ➤ USE PROPS HERE!!!

Galatians 6:7 (KJV) Be not deceived; God is not mocked: for whatsoever a man soweth, that shall he also reap.

(4)Jesus will not draw nigh unto you until you draw nigh to Him.

James 4:8 (KJV) _Draw nigh to God, and he will draw nigh to you._ Cleanse your hands, ye sinners; and purify your hearts, ye double minded.

- ➤ God is a gentleman…
- ➤ He will not force himself on you…
- ➤ He will not make you do what you don't want to do…
- ➤ You have to be willing to trust and obey Him to reap the benefits…
- ➤ Draw close to God and watch how He will hover over you!!!

Matthew 7:11-12 (KJV) If ye then, being evil, know _how to give good gifts unto your children, how much more shall your Father_ which is in heaven _give good things to them that ask him?_ [12] Therefore all things whatsoever _ye would that men should do to you, do ye even so to them:_ for this is the law and the prophets.

__THERE ARE SOMETHINGS THAT GOD WANTS TO DO...BUT HE IS WAITING ON YOU... ARE YOU READY TO OBEY AND BE BLESSED????__

40

STOP POUTING AND START SHOUTING

PROPS:
HAVE ON THE SCREEN A CLIP OF A
CARTOON CHILD CRYING WITH TEARS
FALLING TO THE GROUND WHILE HE IS
WIPING HIS EYES... YOU WANT THIS ONE
TO BE MOVING... ACTION CARTOON.

NEED SEVERAL SMALL MEGAPHONES
1 LARGE MEGAPHONE FOR THE PLATFORM
A TAPE OF A TRUMPET SOUNDING
AS BACKGROUD FOR THE PROJECTOR-
HAVE POUTERS-CHURCH

After Jonah answered the call and obeyed the calling of God, he got angry when God decided to spare the city of Nineveh.

Jonah 3:10 (NIV) When God saw what they did and how they turned from their evil ways, he had compassion and did not bring upon them the destruction he had threatened.

Jonah 4:1-11 (NIV) But Jonah was greatly displeased and *became angry.* [2] He prayed to the LORD, "O LORD, is this not what I said when I was still at home? That is why I was so quick to flee to Tarshish. *I knew that you are a gracious and compassionate God, slow to anger and abounding in love,* a God who relents from sending calamity. [3] Now, O LORD, *take away my life, for it is better for me to die than to live."* [4] But the LORD replied, *"Have you any right to be angry?"* [5] Jonah went out and sat down at a place east of the city. There he made himself a shelter, sat in its shade and waited to see what would happen to the city. [6] *Then the LORD God provided a vine and made it grow up over Jonah to give shade* for his head to ease his discomfort, and *Jonah was very happy about the vine.* [7] But at dawn the next day God provided a worm, which chewed the vine so that it withered. [8] When the sun rose, God provided a scorching east wind, and the sun blazed on Jonah's head so that he grew faint. He wanted to die, and said, "It would be better for me to die than to live." [9] But God said to Jonah, "Do you have a right to be angry about the vine?" "I do," he said. "I am angry enough to die." [10] But the LORD said, "You have been concerned about this vine, though you did not tend it or make it grow. It sprang up overnight and died overnight. [11] But Nineveh has more than a hundred and twenty thousand people who cannot tell their right hand from their left, and many cattle as well. Should I not be concerned about that great city?"

- We need to practice shouting
- We need to understand the purpose of the shout
- A SHOUT....will bring you out

LETS TRY IT:

- Tomorrow you go in to your job and your boss says "You are Fired" .
  SHOUT
- Tomorrow you open a letter and....The house is being repossessed. .
  SHOUT
- Tomorrow the doctor gives you a bad report
  SHOUT
- Tomorrow you get pulled over for speeding
  SHOUT
- Tomorrow you get served with divorce papers
  SHOUT

Joshua 6:1-5 (NIV) Now Jericho was tightly shut up because of the Israelites. No one went out and no one came in. [2] Then the LORD said to Joshua, "See, I have delivered Jericho into your hands, along with its king and its fighting men. [3] March around the city once with all the armed men. Do this for six days. [4] Have seven priests carry trumpets of rams' horns in front of the ark. On the seventh day, march around the city seven times, with the priests blowing the trumpets. [5] When you hear them sound a long blast on

the trumpets, have *all the people give a loud shout;* then the wall of the city will collapse and the people will go up, every man straight in."

Joshua 6:7-11 (NIV) And he ordered the people, "Advance! March around the city, with the armed guard going ahead of the ark of the LORD." [8] When Joshua had spoken to the people, the seven priests carrying the seven trumpets before the LORD went forward, blowing their trumpets, and the ark of the Lord's covenant followed them. [9] The armed guard marched ahead of the priests who blew the trumpets, and the rear guard followed the ark. All this time the trumpets were sounding. [10] But Joshua had commanded the people, "Do not give a war cry, do not raise your voices, do not say a word until the day I tell you to shout. *Then shout!"* [11] So he had the ark of the LORD carried around the city, circling it once. Then the people returned to camp and spent the night there.

Joshua 6:14-16 (NIV) So on the second day they marched around the city once and returned to the camp. They did this for six days. [15] On the seventh day, they got up at daybreak and marched around the city seven times in the same manner, except that on that day they circled the city seven times. [16] The seventh time around, when the priests sounded the trumpet blast, (TRUMPET SOUNDS OVER THE SPEAKERS) Joshua commanded the people, *"Shout!* For the LORD has given you the city!

Joshua 6:20 (NIV) When the trumpets sounded, *the people shouted,* and at the sound of the trumpet, when the people gave a loud shout, the wall collapsed; so every man charged straight in, and they took the city.

WHEN YOU HEAR THE TRUMPET BLOW...YOU NEED TO LEARN TO SHOUT....

(TRUMPET SOUNDS OVER THE SPEAKERS)

WHOSE REPORT SHALL WE BELIEVE.... WE SHALL BELIEVE THE REPORT OF THE LORD.....

(TRUMPET SOUNDS OVER THE SPEAKERS)

Ezra 3:10-13 (NIV) When the builders laid the foundation of the temple of the LORD, the priests in their vestments and with trumpets, and the Levites (the sons of Asaph) with cymbals, took their places to praise the LORD, as prescribed by David king of Israel. [11] With praise and thanksgiving they sang to the LORD: "He is good; his love to Israel endures forever." And all *the people gave a great shout of praise to the LORD,* because the foundation of the house of the LORD was laid. [12] But many of the older priests and

Levites and family heads, who had seen the former temple, wept aloud when they saw the foundation of this temple being laid, while many others shouted for joy. [13] No one could distinguish *the sound of the shouts of joy* from the sound of weeping, because the people made so much noise. And the sound was heard far away.

41

Struck down.... But LIFTED UP!!!

PROPS:
YOU NEED A LIONS DEN.... YOU NEED A BIG LION TO PUT IN THE MIDST OF IT.

2 Corinthians 4:5-10 (NIV) **For we do not preach ourselves, but Jesus Christ as Lord, and ourselves as your servants for Jesus' sake.** [6] **For God, who said, "Let light shine out of darkness," made his light shine in our hearts to give us the light of the knowledge of the glory of God in the face of Christ.** [7] **But we have this treasure in jars of clay to show that this all-surpassing power is from God and not from us.** [8] *We are hard pressed on every side, but not crushed; perplexed, but not in despair;* [9] *persecuted, but not abandoned; struck down, but not destroyed.* [10] **We always carry around in our body the death of Jesus, so that the life of Jesus may also be revealed in our body.**

DANIEL WAS LIFTED UP...TO GET STRUCK DOWN...TO GET LIFTED BACK UP AGAIN...BUT THIS TIME EVEN HIGHER.

Daniels 6:1 (NIV) It pleased _Darius_ to appoint 120 satraps to rule throughout the kingdom, [2] with three administrators over them, one of whom was Daniel. The satraps were made accountable to them so that the king might not suffer loss. [3] Now _Daniel so distinguished himself among the administrators and the satraps by his exceptional qualities that the king planned to set him over the whole kingdom._ [4] At this, the administrators and the satraps tried to find grounds for _charges against Daniel_ in his conduct of government affairs, but _they were unable to do so._ They could find no corruption in him, because _he was trustworthy and neither corrupt nor negligent._ [5] Finally these men said, "_We will never find any basis for charges against this man Daniel unless it has something to do with the law of his God._" [6] So the administrators and the satraps went as a group to the king and said: "O King Darius, live forever! [7] The royal administrators, prefects, satraps, advisers and governors have all agreed that the king should issue an edict and enforce the decree that _anyone who prays to any god or man during the next thirty days, except to you, O king, shall be thrown into the lions' den._ [8] Now, O king, issue the decree and put it in writing so that it cannot be altered--in accordance with the laws of the Medes and Persians, which cannot be repealed." [9] _So King Darius put the decree in writing._ [10] Now when Daniel learned that the decree had been published, he went home to his upstairs room where the windows opened toward Jerusalem. *Three times a day he got down on his knees and prayed, giving thanks to his God, just as he had done before.* [11] Then these men went as a group and found Daniel praying and asking God for help. [12] So they went to the king and spoke to him about his royal decree: "Did you not publish a decree that during the next thirty days anyone who prays to any god or man except to you, O king, would be thrown into the lions' den?" The king answered, "The decree stands--in accordance with the laws of the Medes and Persians, which cannot be repealed." [13] Then they said to the king, *"Daniel, who is one of the exiles from Judah, pays no attention to you,* O king, or to the decree you put in writing. He still prays three times a day." [14] *When the king heard this, he was greatly distressed; he was determined to rescue Daniel and made every effort until sundown to save him.* [15] Then the men went as a group to the king and said to him, "Remember, O king, that according to the law of the Medes and Persians no decree or edict that the king issues can be changed." [16] So the king gave the order, and they brought Daniel and threw him into the lions' den. The king said to Daniel, "May your God, whom you serve continually, rescue you!" [17] A stone was brought and placed over the mouth of the den, and the king sealed it with his own signet ring and with the rings of his nobles, so that Daniel's situation might not be changed. [18] *Then the king returned to his palace and spent the night without eating and without any entertainment being brought to him. And he could not sleep.* [19] At the first light of dawn, *the king got up and hurried to the lions' den.* [20] When he came near the den, he called to Daniel in an anguished voice, *"Daniel, servant of the living God, has your God, whom you serve continually, been able to rescue you from the lions?"* [21] *Daniel answered, "O king, live forever!* [22] *My God sent his angel, and he shut the mouths of the lions. They have not hurt me*, because I was found innocent in his sight. Nor have I ever done any wrong before you, O king." [23] The king was overjoyed and gave orders to lift Daniel out of the den. And when Daniel was lifted from the den, *no wound was found on him, because he had trusted in his God.*

[24] *At the king's command, the men who had falsely accused Daniel were brought in and thrown into the lions' den, along with their wives and children.* And before *they reached the floor of the den, the lions overpowered them and crushed all their bones.* [25] Then King Darius wrote to all the peoples, nations and men of every language throughout the land: *"May you prosper greatly*! [26] "I issue a decree that in every part of my kingdom people must fear and reverence the God of Daniel. "For he is the living God and he endures forever; his kingdom will not be destroyed, his dominion will never end. [27] He rescues and he saves; he performs signs and wonders in the heavens and on the earth. He has rescued Daniel from the power of the lions." [28] *So Daniel prospered during*

the reign of Darius and the reign of Cyrus the Persian.

➢ Darius sets up 120- Satraps-or colonies that was ruled by their own governor.
➢ With 3 administrators to oversee the 120 colonies
➢ One of which would be Daniel
➢ Daniel was so distinguished…. That it was the plan to make him
➢ Ruler over the entire kingdom
➢ In that jealousy rose up

Matthew 22:44 (NIV) **'"The Lord said to my Lord: "Sit at my right hand until _I put your enemies under your feet._"'**

Isaiah 54:17 (KJV) **_No weapon that is formed against thee shall prosper_; and every tongue that shall rise against thee in judgment thou shalt condemn. This is the heritage of the servants of the LORD, and their righteousness is of me, saith the LORD.**

Deuteronomy 28:7 (NIV) **The LORD will grant that _the enemies who rise up against you will be defeated before you. They will come at you from one direction but flee from you in seven._**

Psalms 68:1 (NIV) **…May God arise, _may his enemies be scattered_…**

JESUS TOO…WAS STRUCK DOWN…BUT WAS LIFTED UP…

> THEY THOUGHT WHEN THE STRUCK HIM DOWN TO THE GRAVE IT WAS OVER…. BUT
> IT WAS ONLY THE BEGINNING.
> HE WAS RAISED UP FOR THE WHOLE WORLD TO SEE!!!
> DON'T GIVE UP…EVEN IF YOU ARE DOWN

Jeremiah 29:11 (NIV) For I know the plans I have for you," declares the LORD, "plans to prosper you and not to harm you, plans to give you hope and a future.

42

Swallowing Camels

Props:
You need a life size camel on the platform with me. Also, you need cut out paper camels to be passed out. On the camels- "Swallowing Camels- Matthew 23:24"

How many of you hate hypocrisy?

- One place you don't want to see it is in the church
- You hear of stories that just make you sick
- Pastors falling from Grace
- A saint of God cheating on their taxes
- A missionary or evangelist that skips town with the money
- A little white lie….
- These are all stories of Hypocrisy.

JESUS HATES IT!!!

- He wants us to live with a pure heart

247

- ➢ Right motives
- ➢ And up right actions

JESUS let the Scribes and Pharisees have it for "Extreme Hypocrisy.

I have often heard people say... I am not going to church with a bunch of hypocrites. How dumb is that statement. What they are saying is... I won't go to church with them... but I WILL go to HELL with them.

Let go to the Word of GOD: This morning...I am going to do something that I have never done in my 23 years of ministry... I am sticking to 1 passage of scripture...we are not going any other place....because I want this to sink in this morning...

Everyone swallow real deep and lets go to the WORD...read with me...

Matthew 23:23-28 (NIV) "Woe to you, teachers of the law and Pharisees, you hypocrites! You give a tenth of your spices-- mint, dill and cummin. But you have neglected *the more important matters of the law--justice, mercy and faithfulness*. You should have practiced the latter, *without neglecting the former.* [24] *You blind guides! You strain out a gnat but swallow a camel.* [25] "Woe to you, teachers of the law and Pharisees, you hypocrites! *You clean the*

outside of the cup and dish, but *<u>inside they are full of greed and self-indulgence.</u>* [26] **Blind Pharisee!** *First clean the inside of the cup and dish, and then the outside also will be clean.* [27] **"Woe to you, teachers of the law and Pharisees, you hypocrites! You are like whitewashed tombs, which look beautiful on the outside but on the inside are full of dead men's bones and everything unclean.** [28] **In the same way,** *on the outside you appear to people as righteous but on the inside you are full of hypocrisy and wickedness.*

I preached a part of the ladies conference this weekend. I gave some states they are overwhelming:

- ➤ In 1972 587,000 abortions in America
- ➤ In 1990 1,430,000 abortions in America
- ➤ But things began to turn around....
- ➤ In 1995 1.2 mil abortions
- ➤ In 1997 1.1 mil abortions
- ➤ In 1999 860,000 abortions
- ➤ In 2000 857,000 abortions
- ➤ In 2001 853,000 abortions
- ➤ IT is time that America turns out of hypocrisy and back to GOD.
- ➤ THE ALARMING THING IS THAT ½ OF THESE ARE IN THE CHURCH...OR WITH CHURCH Backgrounds.
- ➤ And over ½ of these abortions are with women over 25 years of age.

More facts:

- 1/3 of all births in America are to single woman that already lost their men
- 2/5 of all birth are to couples that are living together out of wedlock
- Leaving only 26% of our children being born into a home where both father and mother are present and MARRIED.
- Facts are that more than 2/3 of our high school girls are sexually active at a rate of 63%
- While boys in high school are equally active in sexual activity, but with a less percentage than girls at 60%.

Let's talk hypocrisy!!!

- While we sit and complain that we are too hot or too cold…(gnat)…while our society is corrupt in immortal conduct and we say nothing about it.
- While we complain that we don't like the color scheme in our classroom, while our children are being darkened by sin…
- We complain that the sermon is too long…while we only spend 1 minute and 20 seconds in quality time with our children per day.
- While we complain that the church is getting too much money…while we spend 'trillions of dollars giving abortions'

We have to be careful swatting at our gnats… and swallowing our camels.

I don't care how big my house is and how many souls I win to the Lord in my ministry….. if I loose my children to the world.

I don't care how much money I leave for my children's children are an inheritance… If I don't give them the principles of morals in this world…. Be careful swatting at your gnat….while the camel is going down your throat.

- ➢ Camels don't easily go down your throat
- ➢ It is a pretty horrifying thought
- ➢ In trying to take care of less significant issues … you may overlook the big problem.
- ➢ Choose your battles
- ➢ You may not be able to eliminate all hypocrisy from you life…but you can surely do better!!!
- ➢ Kids were jeans to church or stay at home
- ➢ Kids hip hop in church or step to the dance of the world
- ➢ Try to think of your greatest hypocritical problem that YOU have.
- ➢ You may be straining at gnats…but what camel are you swallowing?

- ➢ KIDS: Don't criticize you parents for hating your music…while you in turn hate theirs.

- ➢ Don't despise your supervisor at work for ignoring you…when you do the same thing when you pass by someone you know and don't want to speak
- ➢ Identify the "CAMEL of HYPOCRISY" in your life.

When you are pointing your finger at someone else, you have 3 more pointing back at you!!

43

TAKE OFF YOUR GRAVE CLOTHES!!!

Props:
You need a team of ladies to be dressed in black
with black hats and veils over their
face…mourning.

Today I want to talk about redemption!!! How many of you are glad that you have been redeemed???

Galatians 2:20 (NIV) I have been crucified with Christ and I no longer live, but Christ lives in me. The life I live in the body, *I live by faith in the Son of God, who loved me and gave himself for me.*

1 Corinthians 6:19-20 (NIV) Do you not know that your body is a temple of the Holy Spirit, who is in you, whom you have received from God? You are not your own; [20] _you were bought at a price_. Therefore honor God with your body.

Philippians 1:21 (NIV) For to me, to live is Christ and to die is gain.

John 11:1-4 (NIV) Now a man named *Lazarus* was sick. He was from Bethany, the village of Mary and her sister Martha. [2] This Mary, whose brother Lazarus now lay sick, was the same one who poured perfume on the Lord and wiped his feet with her hair. [3] So the sisters sent word to Jesus, "Lord, the one you love is sick." [4] When he heard this, Jesus said, "_This sickness will not end in death_. No, _it is for God's glory so that God's Son may be glorified through it._"

John 11:11-16 (NIV) After he had said this, he went on to tell them, "Our friend Lazarus has fallen asleep; but I am going there to wake him up." [12] His disciples replied, "Lord, if he sleeps, he will get better." [13] Jesus had been speaking of his death, but his disciples thought he meant natural sleep. [14] So then he told them plainly, "Lazarus is dead, [15] and for your sake I am glad I was not there, so *that you may believe*. But let us go to him." [16] Then Thomas said to the rest of the disciples, "Let us also go, that we may die with him."

THE DISCIPLES NEED TO: TAKE OFF THEIR GRAVE CLOTHES!!!
- ➢ Too many church folks are walking around in their grave clothes
- ➢ Too many church folks look like they been beaten down and left for dead.

- ➤ Too many church folks…talk about how bad it is…
- ➤ Too many church folks … are talking about how hard it is
- ➤ Too many church folks… are too up and too down…
- ➤ Too many church folks… are walking around with their head in the clouds…
- ➤ It IS TIME THAT WE TAKE OUR GRAVE CLOTHES OFF…
- ➤ AND PUT OUR PRAISE CLOTHES ON!!!!

LETS TALK ABOUT SOMEONE…THAT PEOPLE PUT GRAVE CLOTHES ON…EVEN THOUGH…JESUS SAID…THEY NOT DEAD…

- ➤ We try to kill people before it is time
- ➤ We try to bury them before they are dead…
- ➤ We gotta TAKE OFF THOSE GRAVE CLOTHES…AND LIVE!!

John 11:20-27 (NIV) When Martha heard that Jesus was coming, she went out to meet him, but Mary stayed at home. [21] "Lord," Martha said to Jesus, "if you had been here, my brother would not have died. [22] But I know that even now God will give you whatever you ask." [23] Jesus said to her, "Your brother will rise again." [24] Martha answered, "I know he will rise again in the resurrection at the last day." [25] Jesus said to her, "*I am the resurrection and the life. He*_

who believes in me will live, even though he dies; [26] and whoever lives and believes in me will never die. Do you believe this?" [27] "Yes, Lord," she told him, "I believe that you are the Christ, the Son of God, who was to come into the world."

THEN TAKE OFF YOUR GRAVE CLOTHES!!!

John 11:38-44 (NIV)   Jesus, once more deeply moved, came to the tomb. It was a cave with a stone laid across the entrance. [39] "Take away the stone," he said. "But, Lord," said Martha, the sister of the dead man, "by this time there is *a bad odor*, for he has been there four days." [40] Then Jesus said, "*Did I not tell you that if you believed, you would see the glory of God?*" [41] So they took away the stone. Then Jesus looked up and said, "Father, I thank you that you have heard me. [42] I knew that you always hear me, but I said this for the benefit of the people standing here, *that they may believe that you sent me.*" [43] When he had said this, Jesus called in a loud voice, "Lazarus, come out!" [44] *The dead man came out*, his hands and feet wrapped with strips of linen, and a cloth around his face. Jesus said to them, "*Take off the grave clothes and let him go.*"

➤ Some of you have been in your grave clothes so long…you have began to stink!
➤ You need to hear…that it is time to take off…those old clothes…
➤ Cuz the Old Man is dead…

- He paid the price that I could have life and to have it more abundantly.
- He paid the price…that I could hold my head up high with dignity and not shame…
- Who are we to stay in the past…when Jesus paid for our future!!!

Romans 3:22-26 (NIV) This righteousness from God comes *through faith in Jesus Christ to all who believe*. There is no difference, [23] for all have sinned and fall short of the glory of God, [24] and are justified freely by his grace through the redemption that came by Christ Jesus. [25] God presented him as a sacrifice of atonement, through faith in his blood. He did this to demonstrate his justice, because in his forbearance he had left the sins committed beforehand unpunished-- [26] he did it to demonstrate his justice at the present time, so as to be just and the one who justifies those who have faith in Jesus.

- I have been redeemed from my grave clothes…through the power of Gods might.
- I am so glad that he brought me out …
- He set my feet upon a solid foundation
- He loved me when I was unlovable
- He never gave up on me…
- He REDEEMED ME!!!

44

The Garbage of Gossip

Props –
You need what looks like a campfire that has
gone out…(maybe sit the fogger up under some
concrete mix, so a little steam comes up and
some small burnt edges of wood)
You will need LOTS of Trash bags piled up. At
least 30-40. Give all the adults a garbage bag
when they come in.
On the bag- *"Deposit all trash talk here before
leaving" Proverbs 26:20-22.*

Proverbs 26:20-22 (NIV) *Without wood a fire
goes out*; *without gossip a quarrel dies
down.* [21] As charcoal to embers and as wood
to fire, so is a quarrelsome man for kindling
strife. [22] *The words of a gossip are like
choice morsels; they go down to a man's
inmost parts*.

➤ This is not what is referred to in the Bible as
…stir up the gifts…

Gossip = (1) Rumor or reports (2) Chatty talk (3) A personal who habitually reveals personal or sensational facts.

➢ Gossip starts with an UNHEALTHY INTEREST into someone else's business.
➢ Gossip seeks an UNINVITED INVOLVEMENT in someone else's concerns.
➢ Gossip spreads as an UNWARRANTED INFORMING of someone else's thoughts.

THE DELIGHT IN GOSSIP:

Proverbs 26:22 (NIV) *__The words of a gossip are like choice morsels; they go down to a man's inmost parts__*.

➢ Gossip is one thing that has to be bad in order to be good!
➢ Old saying: If you cant say anything good about someone…don't say anything at all… but
➢ A gossip says: If you can't say anything good about a person…LET'S HEAR IT!!
➢ The only time that people dislike gossip…is when it is about them.

Paul Says:
2 Corinthians 12:20 (NIV) For *I am afraid that when I come I may not find you as I want you to be,* and you may not find me as you want

me to be. I fear that there may be quarreling, jealousy, outbursts of anger, factions, slander, _gossip_, arrogance and disorder.

Gossip damages in many ways:
 1. It betrays
 Proverbs 11:13 (NIV) A gossip betrays a confidence, but a trustworthy man keeps a secret.

 2. It separates
 Proverbs 16:28 (NIV) A perverse man stirs up dissension, and a gossip separates close friends.

GOSSIP CAUSES:
 ➤ IRREPARABLE DAMAGE
 ➤ IRRESOLVABLE DIVISION
 ➤ ISOLATION AND DETACHMENT

The Bible says that we must get rid of GOSSIP

Ephesians 4:31 (NIV) _Get rid of all bitterness, rage and anger, brawling and slander, along with every form of malice_.(or gossip)

FOUR GREAT QUESTIONS TO ASK SOMEONE THAT IS GOSSIPING TO YOU:
 1. Why are you telling me this?
 2. Where did you hear this from?
 3. Did you verify it with the one that it is about?
 4. Can I quote you freely and use your name?

Proverbs 11:13 (NIV) _A gossip betrays a confidence_, but a trustworthy man keeps a secret.

Proverbs 16:28 (NIV) A perverse man stirs up dissension, and _a gossip separates close friends._

Leviticus 19:16 (NIV) "_'Do not go about spreading slander (gossip) among your people_. '"Do not do anything that endangers your neighbor's life. I am the LORD.

Colossians 3:8 (NIV) _But now you must rid yourselves of all such things_ as these: anger, rage, malice, slander,(gossip) and filthy language from your lips.

James 4:11 (NIV) Brothers, _do not slander one another_. Anyone who speaks against his brother or judges him speaks against the law and judges it. When you judge the law, you are not keeping it, but sitting in judgment on it.

1 Peter 2:1 (NIV) Therefore, _rid yourselves of all malice and all deceit, hypocrisy, envy, and slander (GOSSIP) of every kind_.

Titus 3:1-2 (NIV) Remind the people to be subject to rulers and authorities, to be obedient, to _be ready to do whatever is good,_ [2] _to slander (gossip about) no one,_ to be peaceable and considerate, and to show true humility toward all men.

45

THE LEFT OVER CRUMBS

Props:
You will need mouse traps, and one REALY BIG rat trap on platform. You can use flat panel doors to make one. You will need a nice, cartoon type power point with the story of the chicken, pig, cow and mouse.

A mouse looked through the crack in the wall to see the farmer and his wife open a package. "What food might this contain?" He was devastated to discover it was a mousetrap.

Retreating to the farmyard, the mouse proclaimed the warning. "There is a mousetrap in the house! There is a mousetrap in the house!"

The chicken clucked and scratched, raised her head and said, "Mr. Mouse, I can tell this is a grave concern to you, but it is of no consequence to me. I cannot be bothered by it."

The mouse turned to the pig and told him, "There is a mousetrap in the house."

The pig sympathized, but said, "I am so very sorry, Mr. Mouse, but there is nothing I can do about it but pray. Be assured you are in my prayers."

The mouse turned to the cow. She said, "Wow, Mr. Mouse. I'm sorry for you, but it's no skin off my nose."

So, the mouse returned to the house, head down and rejected, to face the farmer's mousetrap alone.

That very night a sound was heard throughout the house -- like the sound of a mousetrap catching its prey.

The farmer's wife rushed to see what was caught. In the darkness, she did not see it was a venomous snake whose tail the trap had caught.

The snake bit the farmer's wife. The farmer rushed her to the hospital, and she returned home with a fever. Everyone knows you treat a fever with fresh chicken soup, so the farmer took his hatchet to the farmyard for the soup's main ingredient. [The mouse ate all the leftover crumbs]

But his wife's sickness continued, so friends and neighbors came to sit with her around the clock. To feed them, the farmer butchered the pig. [The mouse ate all the leftover crumbs]

The farmer's wife did not get well; she died. So many people came for her funeral, the farmer had the cow slaughtered to provide enough meat for all of them. [The mouse ate all the leftover crumbs]

So, the next time you hear someone is facing a problem and think it doesn't concern you, remember -- when one of us is threatened, we are all at risk. [And the mouse eats all the leftover crumbs]

Cain asked a question in Genesis 4…that we still ask today:

Genesis 4:1-9(NIV) Adam lay with his wife Eve, and she became pregnant and gave birth to Cain. She said, "With the help of the LORD I have brought forth a man." [2] Later she gave birth to his brother Abel. Now Abel kept flocks, and Cain worked the soil. [3] In the course of time Cain brought some of the fruits of the soil as an offering to the LORD. [4] But Abel brought fat portions from some of the firstborn of his flock. The LORD looked with favor on Abel and his offering, [5] but on Cain and his offering he did not look with favor. So Cain was very angry, and his face was downcast. [6] Then the LORD said to Cain, "Why are you angry? Why is your face downcast? [7] If you do what is right, will you not be accepted? But if you do not do what is right, *sin is crouching at your door*; it desires to have you, but *you must master it*." [8] Now Cain said to his brother Abel, "Let's go out to the field." And while they were in the field, *Cain attacked his brother Abel and killed him.* [9] Then the LORD said to Cain, "Where is your brother Abel?" "I don't know," he replied. "_Am I my brother's keeper_?"

In the book of Genesis, Cain said this about Able, his brother, to our God: "Am I my

265

brother's keeper?" The answer to that question.... Is YES!!

1 Corinthians 8:8-13 (NIV) But food does not bring us near to God; we are no worse if we do not eat, and no better if we do. [9] Be careful, however, that the exercise of your freedom does _not become a stumbling block to the weak._ [10] For if anyone with a weak conscience sees you who have this knowledge eating in an idol's temple, won't he be emboldened to eat what has been sacrificed to idols? [11] So this weak brother, for whom Christ died, is destroyed by your knowledge. [12] _When you sin against your brothers in this way and wound their weak conscience, you sin against Christ._ [13] Therefore, _if what I eat causes my brother to fall into sin, I will never eat meat again_, so that _I will not cause him to fall_.

Romans 14:13 (NIV) Therefore _let us stop passing judgment on one another._ Instead, make up your mind _not to put any stumbling block or obstacle in your brother's way_.

The answer to the age long asked question.... AM I MY BROTHERS KEEPER.... THE ANSWER IS

YES!!!

2 Corinthians 6:1-10 (NIV) As God's fellow workers we urge you not to receive God's grace in vain. [2] For he says, "In the time of my favor I heard you, and in the day of salvation I helped you." I tell you, _now is the_

time of God's favor, now is the day of salvation. ³ _We put no stumbling block in anyone's path_, so that our ministry will not be discredited. ⁴ Rather, as servants of God we commend ourselves in every way: in great endurance; in troubles, hardships and distresses; ⁵ in beatings, imprisonments and riots; in hard work, sleepless nights and hunger; ⁶ in purity, understanding, patience and kindness; in the Holy Spirit and in sincere love; ⁷ in truthful speech and in the power of God; with weapons of righteousness in the right hand and in the left; ⁸ through glory and dishonor, bad report and good report; genuine, yet regarded as impostors; ⁹ known, yet regarded as unknown; dying, and yet we live on; beaten, and yet not killed; ¹⁰ sorrowful, yet always rejoicing; poor, yet making many rich; having nothing, and _yet possessing everything_.

We are all involved in this journey called life. We must keep an eye out for one another and make an extra effort to encourage one another.

Galatians 6:1-3 (NIV) Brothers, if someone is caught in a sin, _you who are spiritual should restore him gently_. But _watch yourself_, or you also may be tempted. ² Carry each other's burdens, and in this way you will fulfill the law of Christ. ³ If anyone thinks he is something when he is nothing, he deceives himself.

Hebrews 3:12-13 (NIV) See to it, brothers, that none of you has a sinful, unbelieving heart that turns away from the living God. [13] But *encourage one another daily,* as long as it is called Today, so that none of you may be hardened by sin's deceitfulness.

46

TOO MUCH SALVATION!

OK NOW, You say Pastor you have lost your mind on this one!!!

PROPS:
You need an BIG inflatable whale, a pail, a jail, a hell, a veil...5 separate scenes. (hell can be from the pool with just the lights, flames and fogger...veil...needs to be a king blanket that can be ripped down the middle (needs to be hanging)

Luke 19:1-9 (NIV) Jesus entered Jericho and was passing through. [2] A man was there by the name of Zacchaeus; he was a chief tax collector and was wealthy. [3] He wanted to see who Jesus was, but being a short man he could not, because of the crowd. [4] So he ran ahead and climbed a sycamore-fig tree to see him, since Jesus was coming that way. [5] When Jesus reached the spot, he looked up and said to him, "Zacchaeus, come down immediately. I must stay at your house

today." [6] **So he came down at once and welcomed him gladly.** [7] **All the people saw this and began to mutter, "He has gone to be the guest of a 'sinner.'"** [8] **But Zacchaeus stood up and said to the Lord, "Look, Lord! Here and now I give half of my possessions to the poor, and if I have cheated anybody out of anything, I will pay back four times the amount."** [9] **Jesus said to him, "Today salvation has come to this house…**

You can have too much Salvation for <u>some of those that are roundabout you</u>; like your job, school or even your kin folks that think you're a religious whacko - *even some in your own church family.*

Now let me explain, we all have the same amount of Salvation but some folks really express their Salvation through shouting and tears and joy and when these excited Christians get in a quiet Church the dead ones say the live ones has **TOO MUCH SALVATION** for me…

I heard a story of a young overly excited new Christian that got to shouting in a small town quiet church…the ushers told him that he would have to sit down and be quiet…he told them… I found religion… the usher looked at him and said… "Well, you didn't find it here….so sit down…"

I want to be identified with those that are labeled as having to **TOO MUCH SALVATION** *AMEN !* *AMEN !*

So lets see some places where there was TOO MUCH SALVATION
There was too much Salvation for the WHALE !!!

Now you know the story of the Whale in Jonah Ch 2.

> The Whale was ok...with eating Jonah,.... until V. 9
> When Jonah said "Salvation is of the LORD" the whale could not handle that testimony so he vomited up Jonah.

Jonah 2:9-10 (NIV) But I, with a song of thanksgiving, will sacrifice to you. What I have vowed I will make good. *Salvation comes from the LORD*." ¹⁰ And the LORD commanded the fish, and *it vomited Jonah onto dry land*.

But Like Festus in Acts 27:24 said to Paul, "you have **TOO MUCH SALVATION** until its driving you crazy"

There was too much Salvation for the Jail !!!

In Acts 16, Paul and Silas, bleeding and in pain but enjoying Salvation, they just had **TOO MUCH SALVATION** to stop praising GOD.

> **Acts 16:25-31(NIV) About midnight Paul and Silas were praying and singing hymns to God, and the other prisoners were listening to them. [26] Suddenly there was such a violent earthquake that the foundations of the prison were shaken. At once all the prison doors flew open, and everybody's chains came loose. [27] The jailer woke up, and when he saw the prison doors open, he drew his sword and was about to kill himself because he thought the prisoners had escaped. [28] But Paul shouted, "Don't harm yourself! We are all here!" [29] The jailer called for lights, rushed in and fell trembling before Paul and Silas. [30] He then brought them out and asked, "Sirs, what must I do to be saved?" [31] They replied, "Believe in the Lord Jesus, and you will be saved--you and your household."**

➢ We need our prisoners today…to find…TOO MUCH SALVATION for the prisons to hold them
➢ We need an out pouring in our jails and prisons…but will never find it until we experience it in the church…
➢ Paul and Silas had it…and the JAIL couldn't hold it
➢ That is why many of us are stuck in our problems…
➢ They seem to BIG for us…and they are…

➤ But when SALVATION takes over all that changes!!!

There was too much Salvation in The PAIL !!!

John 4: The woman at the well with her pail, went home with the whole well after JESUS told her that her bucket had a hole in it.

➤ JESUS had **TOO MUCH SALVATION** to offer her.
➤ It didn't matter if she was a Samaritan
➤ OR that she had been married five times.
➤ This crowd now days would have thrown her down the well but that shows this generation doesn't have **TOO MUCH SALVATION.**

John 4:11-14 (NIV)   "Sir," the woman said, "you have nothing to draw with and the well is deep. Where can you get this living water? ^{12} Are you greater than our father Jacob, who gave us the well and drank from it himself, as did also his sons and his flocks and herds?" ^{13} Jesus answered, "Everyone who drinks this water will be thirsty again, ^{14} but whoever drinks the water I give him will never thirst. Indeed, the water I give him will become in him a spring of water welling up to eternal life."

You need to:

- Drop your pail
- Jumped the rail
- And hit the trail

There's too much Salvation to TELL !!

The choir used to sing a song…that says…It is so good… I just can't tell it all…. So good…I just cant tell it all…so good…so good…I just can't tell it all!!!

- How many of you have ever felt that way?
- God has been so good to me since salvation….
- I JUST CANT TELL IT ALL!!!

There's too much Salvation to SELL !!!

- Bill Gates or Wal-Mart cannot buy what you and I have and it was given freely.
- Money and items…could never amount to what Salvation brings…
- Money is good and nice to have… it buys you houses and cars… food and clothing…
- But it can only give you peace and joy temporarily…
- You say… I WOULD LIKE TO TRY…
- Notice all the stars that has filed bankruptcy and has lost their marriages over money
- Notice those that have taken their lives when the stock market crashed…

> ONLY SALVATION THROUGH JESUS CAN GIVE REAL PEACE AND HAPPINESS!!!

Too much Salvation for HELL !!!!

Hell has a problem with us children of GOD because we just have **TO MUCH SALVATION** for that place.

> Jesus went down to Hell… and took the keys from the Enemy…

1 Corinthians 15:55-58 (NIV)   "Where, O death, is your victory? Where, O death, is your sting?" [56] The sting of death is sin, and the power of sin is the law. [57] But thanks be to God! He gives us the victory through our Lord Jesus Christ. [58] Therefore, my dear brothers, stand firm. Let nothing move you. Always give yourselves fully to the work of the Lord, because you know that your labor in the Lord is not in vain.

There was so much Salvation behind that veil !!!!

> Glory to GOD there is a new living way.
> The day that Christ died the veil was rent from top to bottom and the last lamb died.
> Did you know that the JEWS sewed up the veil to stop people from entering in after GOD the Father destroyed that veil. The

Jews would say STOP! STOP! you can't enter in

➢ My friend ever since Calvary JESUS is saying "I opened a new way come In

➢ I have **MUCH SALVATION**

Matthew 27:50-53 (KJV) Jesus, when he had cried again with a loud voice, yielded up the ghost. ^{51} And, behold, the veil of the temple was rent in twain from the top to the bottom; and the earth did quake, and the rocks rent; ^{52} And the graves were opened; and many bodies of the saints which slept arose, ^{53} And came out of the graves after his resurrection, and went into the holy city, and appeared unto many.

So I pray that you can see there was to much Salvation for the Whale, Jail, Pail, To Tell, To Sell, For Hell, and the Veil.

47

WARNING!!! THIS IS ONLY A TEST!!!

Props:
Have the Radio Announcement-- "Warning this is only a test" on CD

It appears that many of US have been going through some test this week. Ever since we had our deliverance service, the enemy has been mad.

- ➤ We've been physically sick
- ➤ We've had the bus to break down for our campers…numerous times
- ➤ We've had emergency hospital visits
- ➤ We've had infant deaths
- ➤ We've had floods
- ➤ We've had court hearings
- ➤ We've had arrests

So I have just come to tell you …. That………..

WARNING....THIS IS ONLY A TEST!!!!

James 1:2-3 (NIV) Consider it pure joy, my brothers, whenever you face trials of many kinds, [3] _**because you know that the testing of your faith develops perseverance.**_

Is any one persevering? WEBSTER (1) To persist in a state (2) to undertake in spite of oppositions.

GOD'S TEST TO ABRAHAM

Genesis 22:1-3 (NIV) Some time later God tested Abraham. He said to him, "Abraham!" "Here I am," he replied. [2] Then God said, "Take your son, your only son, Isaac, whom you love, and go to the region of Moriah. Sacrifice him there as a burnt offering on one of the mountains I will tell you about." [3] Early the next morning Abraham got up and saddled his donkey.

➢ I have had a lot of test...but none like Abraham
➢ Abraham had to offer his son to the Lord... through sacrifice
➢ Abraham entered it knowing that it was only a test

GOD'S STRANGE PLAN FOR JOSHUA'S TEST

Joshua 6:3 March around the city once with all the armed men. Do this for six days.

➤ Joshua was being tested for six day to see if he would remain consistent and faithful.
➤ Joshua realized that it was "ONLY A TEST"
➤ Therefore he knew that he couldn't give up...that soon
➤ He would possess the city
➤ What are you wanting to claim

GOD'S TEST WAS NOT FOR ALL-JUST THE STRONG

Judges 7:1-9 (NIV) Early in the morning, Jerub-Baal (that is, Gideon) and all his men camped at the: spring of Harod. The camp of Midian was north of them in the valley near the hill of Moreh. ² The LORD said to Gideon, _"You have too many men_ for me to deliver Midian into their hands. In order that Israel may not boast against me that her own strength has saved her, ³ announce now to the people, _'Anyone who trembles with fear may turn back and leave Mount Gilead.'" So twenty-two thousand men left, while ten thousand remained. ⁴_ But the LORD said to Gideon, "There are still too many men. Take them down to the water, and I will sift them for you there. If I say, 'This one shall go with you,' he shall go; but if I say, 'This one shall not go with you,' he shall not go." ⁵ So Gideon took the men down to the water. There the LORD told him, _"Separate those_

who lap the water with their tongues like a dog from those who kneel down to drink."
⁶ ***Three hundred men lapped with their hands to their mouths***. All the rest got down on their knees to drink. ⁷ The LORD said to Gideon, "***With the three hundred men that lapped I will save you and give the Midianites into your hands. Let all the other men go***, each to his own place."(Romans 8:31-If God be for us, who can be against us?) ⁸ So Gideon sent the rest of the Israelites to their tents but kept *the three hundred*, who took over the provisions and trumpets of the others. Now the camp of Midian lay below him in the valley. ⁹ During that night the LORD said to Gideon, "Get up, go down against the camp, ***because I am going to give it into your hands.***

- ➢ Gideon was being tested, in his faith.
- ➢ He had 32,000 men
- ➢ Then he went down to 10,000
- ➢ Then to 300
- ➢ His faith had to become strong
- ➢ HE realized, 'THIS WAS ONLY A TEST'

GOD'S TEST MAY COST YOU SOMETHING

1 Kings 17:13 Elijah said to her, "Don't be afraid. Go home and do as you have said. ***But first*** make a small cake of bread for me from what you have and bring it to me, ***and then*** make something for yourself and your son.

GOD'S TEST MAY SEEM TO BE ALOT OF WORK WITH NO BLESSING IN SIGHT

2 Kings 4: 3 Elisha said, "Go around and ask all your neighbors for empty jars. Don't ask for just a few.

CLOSING:

1 Peter 7:7 These have come so that your _faith--of greater worth than gold_, which perishes even though _refined by fire_--may be proved _genuine_ and may _result in praise, glory and honor_ when _Jesus Christ is revealed_.

Our test always has the potential of giving praise unto God and glorifying Him.

48

We are all Mephibosheth's

Props:
You need everyone to have a name tag that say:
HELLO, I'M Mephibosheth

Charis is the Geek word for "Grace," is one of the most difficult Greek words to translate into English. Words like:

➤ Favor
➤ Beauty
➤ Thankfulness
➤ Gratitude
➤ Delight
➤ Kindness
➤ And Benefit

.....................all derive from the root word "GRACE." If we have a tough time translating THIS word, there is no wonder that we struggle to comprehend the concept of "GRACE."

Digging through Scriptures, we can come up with a picture of grace.

- ➢ Grace is ALWAYS tied to the heart and Character of God.
- ➢ In Deuteronomy, we are told that God drove out Israel's enemies, not because Israel deserved his intervention, but because God chose... BY GRACE...to fulfill His word to His nation.
- ➢ In Isaiah, we see that God longed to demonstrate His GRACE to a disobedient nation.
- ➢ In Jeremiah God underlined His GRACE by promising to bring Israel back from captivity.

GRACE IS GOD'S CHARACTER DEMONSTRATED IN UNDESERVED LOVE!!!! In fact... Grace IS GOD!!! It is His character illustrated in our lives with the scrawled signature at the cross.

GRACE=God giving us something we do not deserve
- ➢ Life
- ➢ Another opportunity
- ➢ Success
- ➢ Eternal Salvation

MERCY=God not giving us what we deserve.
- ➢ Health over Aids
- ➢ Life over death in a fatal wreck

- Piece of mind over nervous breakdown
- Faithfulness over our abandonment

The truth is… we are all Mephibosheth's.
WE DIDN'T DESERVE GRACE OR MERCY….

- After David became King, he had a right to kill any of Saul's remaining family
- There had been a rivalry between the two families for years.
- David now becomes king and takes the throne….let's read:

2 Samuel 9:1-11 (NIV) David asked, "Is there anyone still left of the house of Saul to whom I can show kindness for Jonathan's sake?" [2] Now there was a servant of Saul's household named Ziba. They called him to appear before David, and the king said to him, "Are you Ziba?" "Your servant," he replied. [3] The king asked, "Is there no one still left of the house of Saul to whom I can show God's kindness?" Ziba answered the king, "There is still a son of Jonathan; he is crippled in both feet." [4] "Where is he?" the king asked. Ziba answered, "He is at the house of Makir son of Ammiel in Lo Debar." [5] So King David had him brought from Lo Debar, from the house of Makir son of Ammiel. [6] When Mephibosheth son of Jonathan, the son of Saul, came to David, he bowed down to pay him honor. David said, "Mephibosheth!" "Your servant," he replied. [7] "Don't be afraid," David said to him, "for I will surely

285

show you kindness for the sake of your father Jonathan. I will restore to you all the land that belonged to your grandfather Saul, and you will always eat at my table." [8] Mephibosheth bowed down and said, "What is your servant, that you should notice a dead dog like me?" [9] Then the king summoned Ziba, Saul's servant, and said to him, "I have given your master's grandson everything that belonged to Saul and his family. [10] You and your sons and your servants are to farm the land for him and bring in the crops, so that your master's grandson may be provided for. And Mephibosheth, grandson of your master, will always eat at my table." (Now Ziba had fifteen sons and twenty servants.) [11] Then Ziba said to the king, "Your servant will do whatever my lord the king commands his servant to do." So Mephibosheth ate at David's table like one of the king's sons.

➢ David chose, that after he became king of what to do with a longtime family feud
➢ It was between the house of David and the House of Saul
➢ Instead of killing Saul's family, which he had a right to do, he chose to respond with kindness.
➢ He sought after who was left in Saul's family.
➢ Mephibosheth, a grandson of Saul was still living.
➢ He was crippled in both feet.

- He was brought to David's house and to David's table to eat

- David's kindness resembles God's Grace to us
- Even though we did nothing He still forgave us
- Even though we didn't deserve it....He gave it anyways
- Even though we persecuted Him... He still loved us...THAT IS GRACE.

We are creatures that have been drawn to pretty and nice things. We like nice restaurants, elegant shopping malls, roomy homes and sweet-smelling, happy easy-to-know people. We instinctively shun the unlovelies of life. Consequently, we have a terrible time understanding the GRACE OF GOD.

God's GRACE loves when there is nothing good even beneath an awful wrapper. When layer upon layer is removed and all that appears is more ugliness, God loves. It's not that we're such precious darlings that he can't resist loving us. No, God loves us because He's decided that we will be precious to Him. He sent His Son to die on the cross for our ugliness. PERIOD!!!

It's hard to imagine isn't it? It's even harder to accept. We push and tug at ourselves, trying to earn love and attention when the fact is, whatever package we come in, God loves us. Dressing ourselves up with good deeds, advanced degrees and charitable attitudes doesn't increase God's love for us. He simply reaches down into our torn, misshapen world and makes people who are ugly, precious.

Mercy=God not giving us what we deserve

Romans 9:15-18 (NIV) For he says to Moses, "_I will have mercy on whom I have mercy_, and I will have compassion on whom I have compassion." [16] It does not, therefore, depend on man's desire or effort, but on God's mercy. [17] For the Scripture says to Pharaoh: "I raised you up for this very purpose, that I might display my power in you and that my name might be proclaimed in all the earth." [18] _Therefore God has mercy on whom he wants to have mercy,_ and he hardens whom he wants to harden.

Psalms 23 (KJV) A Psalm of David. The LORD is my shepherd; I shall not want. [2] He maketh me to lie down in green pastures: he leadeth me beside the still waters. [3] He restoreth my soul: he leadeth me in the paths of righteousness for his name's sake. [4] Yea, though I walk through the valley of the shadow of death, I will fear no evil: for thou

art with me; thy rod and thy staff they comfort me. [5] Thou preparest a table before me in the presence of mine enemies: thou anointest my head with oil; my cup runneth over. [6] *Surely goodness and* <u>*mercy*</u> *shall follow me* all the days of my life: and I will dwell in the house of the LORD for ever.

➢ I am so glad that God gave me His MERCY and GRACE
➢ I didn't deserve it… but I obtained it.
➢ How many of you all are sitting in places today that you didn't deserve
➢ How many of you have experienced…God's GRACE and MERCY

49

WHAT IS YOUR HOUSE BUILT ON??

PROPS:
You need 3 pigs, a wolf, a straw house, a wood house, and a brick house. Also have to have the story book… "The Three Little Pigs." Also need a small amount of straw, sticks, and bricks…to hold up as you preach.

The Story of the Three Little Pigs

There was an old sow with three little pigs, and as she had not enough to keep them, she sent them out to seek their fortune. The first that went off met a man with a bundle of straw, and said to him, "Please, man, give me that straw to build me a house." Which the man did, and the little pig built a house with it.

Presently came along a wolf, and knocked at the door, and said, "Little pig, little pig, let me come in."

To which the pig answered, "No, no, by the hair of my chiny chin chin."

The wolf then answered to that, "Then I'll huff, and I'll puff, and I'll blow your house in." So he huffed, and he puffed, and he blew his house in, and ate up the little pig.

The second little pig met a man with a bundle of sticks, and said, "Please, man, give me those sticks to build a house." Which the man did, and the pig built his house.

Then along came the wolf, and said, "Little pig, little pig, let me come in."

"No, no, by the hair of my chiny chin chin."

"Then I'll puff, and I'll huff, and I'll blow your house in." So he huffed, and he puffed, and he puffed, and he huffed, and at last he blew the house down, and he ate up the little pig.

The third little pig met a man with a load of bricks, and said, "Please, man, give me those bricks to build a house with." So the man gave him the bricks, and he built his house with them.

So the wolf came, as he did to the other little pigs, and said, "Little pig, little pig, let me come in."

"No, no, by the hair of my chiny chin chin."

"Then I'll huff, and I'll puff, and I'll blow your house in."

> Well, he huffed, and he puffed, and he huffed and he puffed, and he puffed and huffed; but he could *not* get the house down.

Matthew 7:24-27 (NIV) "Therefore everyone who hears these words of mine and puts them into practice is like a wise man who built his house on the rock. [25] The rain came down, the streams rose, and the winds blew and beat against that house; yet it did not fall, because it had its foundation on the rock. [26] But everyone who hears these words of mine and does not put them into practice is like a foolish man who built his house on sand. [27] The rain came down, the streams rose, and the winds blew and beat against that house, and it fell with a great crash."

Matthew 7:24-27 (The Message)

24-25 "These words I speak to you are not incidental additions to your life, homeowner improvements to your standard of living. They are foundational words, words to build a life on. If you work these words into your life, you are like a smart carpenter who built his house on solid rock. Rain poured down, the river flooded, a tornado hit—but nothing moved that house. It was fixed to the rock.

26-27 "But if you just use my words in Bible studies and don't work them into your life, you are like a stupid carpenter who built his house on the sandy beach. When a storm

**rolled in and the waves came up, it collapsed
like a house of cards."**

➤ Often times…we go through life…
➤ Like the little pigs…
➤ Taking short cuts…
➤ That end up costing us BIG!!!

**1 Corinthians 6:19-20 (NIV) Do you not know
that your body is a temple (house) of the
Holy Spirit, who is in you, whom you have
received from God? You are not your own; [20]
you were bought at a price. Therefore honor
God with your body.**

➤ We will take time out of our life…to work on
the outside of our house
➤ We will get weaves
➤ We will buy nice clothes
➤ We will go to the beauty or barber shop
➤ We will get our nails and toes done
➤ We will even treat ourselves to a massage…
➤ BUT….
➤ What about the TEMPLE???
➤ Shouldn't we spend more time on making it
beautiful
➤ With Prayer…making our attitude sweeter
➤ With   Fasting…making   us   more
compassionate
➤ With   Study…Making   ourselves   more
equipped???

I like to compare teaching at church with teaching at school:

> If your child didn't study Math...we would be upset
> If they back talked the teacher or principle...we would be at the school to see what we could do
> If they were not getting knowledge...we would have a problem with that
> We spend countless hours on that with our children every week...
> YET...WHAT ARE WE TEACHING THEM ABOUT THE GOSPEL?

I KNOW YOU SAY...BUT EDUCATION IS GOING TO GET THEM A JOB AND PUT FOOD ON THEIR TABLE... THEY HAVE TO GET GOOD GRADES AND A COLLEGE EDUCATION.... AND I AGREE...

> BUT what more to help them get the education...and obtaining knowledge... and being able to concentrate...than JESUS CHRIST.
> Very rarely do we have someone talk to a Wednesday night or Sunday School teacher about the child's spiritual involvement or learning abilities...
> When in essence it is even more important than ANYTHING ELSE WE DO...

That is when we SETTLE... For a straw or wood house...

> I want my boys to have a great education...
> I want them to be good in sports and to bring home that scholarship]
> BUT I also want them to know that God Gives all wisdom
> AND all Knowledge...
> And the power to make wealth...
> And the power to Heal ...
> And the Power to deliver...
> And the Power to promote...
> And the Power to overcome...
> And if we don't build our house on a SOLID FOUNDATION... it is destined to FALL!!!

FOUNDATION IS THE LIFE SOURCE OF ANY BUILDING... IF THE FOUNDATION IS WEAK...THE HOUSE IS WEAK.. .IF THE FOUNDATION IS WEAK... THE ROOF IS WEAK... IF THE FOUNDATION IS WEAK.... THE WALLS ARE WEAK...WE MUST HAVE A BRICK... SOLID ... STURDY... FOUNDATION...

IF THE LITTLE PIGS FIGURED THIS OUT.... WE SHOULD BE ABLE TO!!!

50

Whose Battle is this?

Props:
You will need a Gun Cabinet, Guns etc, swords… and several military artillery on the screen. Different toy guns etc to pass out to adults that say… *"Whose Battle is this?"* And you need a trumpet.

The Lord Speaks about Babylon:

Jeremiah 50:22-25 (NIV) The noise of battle is in the land, the noise of great destruction! [23] How broken and shattered is the hammer of the whole earth! How desolate is Babylon among the nations! [24] I set a trap for you, O Babylon, and you *were caught before you knew it*; you were found and captured because you opposed the LORD. [25] The LORD has opened his arsenal (storage of arms and military equipment) and brought out the weapons of his wrath, for the Sovereign LORD Almighty has work to do in the land of the Babylonians.

➢ He opened his arsenal

- You don't want God to open His arsenal against you
- It doesn't compare to the Military:
- Machine Guns
- Tanks
- Bombs
- Guns
- And other military artillery

He was getting ready to do an overhaul on Babylon
- Realize, some of you here this morning
- God may have brought you here to give you an overhaul
- You need to obey God… don't make God open his gun cabinet
- You promised God what you were going to do if….
- You promised what you would give him if…

Babylon … was caught in God's disastrous trap.
- God says:
- you were caught before you knew it
- Because you opposed God!
- So… God opened up his gun cabinet
- And shot wrath down upon them.
- And gave them a home makeover!!!!

1 Corinthians 14:8 (NIV) Again, if the trumpet does not sound a clear call, *who will get*

**ready for battle?** (Have someone come up and blow a trumpet.)

> ➢ I am blowing the trumpet for someone today about your battle...
> ➢ IT IS NOT YOURS
> ➢ IF it is... fight it yourself....
> ➢ But if it is not...
> ➢ Give it to the Lord and leave it there!!!

2 Chronicles 20:13-17 (NIV) All the men of Judah, with their wives and children and little ones, stood there before the LORD. ¹⁴ _Then the Spirit of the LORD came upon Jahaziel_ (son of Zechariah, the son of Benaiah, the son of Jeiel, the son of Mattaniah, a Levite and descendant of Asaph,) as he stood in the assembly. ¹⁵ He said: "Listen, King Jehoshaphat and all who live in Judah and Jerusalem! This is what the LORD says to you: 'Do not be afraid or discouraged because of this vast army. _For the battle is not yours, but God's._ ¹⁶ Tomorrow march down against them. They will be climbing up by the Pass of Ziz, and you will find them at the end of the gorge in the Desert of Jeruel. ¹⁷ _You will not have to fight this battle._ Take up your positions; stand _firm and see the deliverance the LORD will give you_, O Judah and Jerusalem. _Do not be afraid; do not be discouraged._ Go out to face them tomorrow, and the LORD will be with you.'"

1 Samuel 17:45-47 (NIV) _David said_ to the Philistine, "You come against me with sword

and spear and javelin, but I come against you in the name of the LORD Almighty, the God of the armies of Israel, whom you have defied. [46] This day the LORD will hand you over to me, and I'll strike you down and cut off your head. Today I will give the carcasses of the Philistine army to the birds of the air and the beasts of the earth, and the whole world will know that there is a God in Israel. [47] *All those gathered here will know that it is not by sword or spear that the LORD saves; for the battle is the Lord's*, and he will give all of you into our hands."

2 Corinthians 10:3-5 (NIV) For though we live in the world, *we do not wage war as the world does.* [4] *The weapons we fight with are not the weapons of the world*. On the contrary, they have divine power to demolish strongholds. [5] We demolish arguments and every pretension that sets itself up against the knowledge of God, and *we take captive every thought to make it obedient to Christ.*

Ephesians 6:10-13 (NIV) Finally, be strong in the Lord and in his mighty power. [11] Put on the full armor of God so that you can take your stand against the devil's schemes. [12] *For our struggle is not against flesh and blood, but against the rulers, against the authorities, against the powers of this dark world and against the spiritual forces of evil* in the heavenly realms. [13] Therefore *put on the full armor of God*, so that when the day of evil comes, you may be able to stand your

ground, and after you have done everything,
to stand.

51

You better watch your ATTITUDE -because God is watching you!!

This morning, I want to conclude a 4 week series on the 4 deadliest sins in the church.

1. Gossip
2. Stubbornness
3. Anger (Temper) and today....
4. ATTITUDE....

WHEN EVER I YELL OUT... "ATTITUDE ADJUSTMENT"... JUMP UP AND SAY... "PRAISE THE LORD!!"

➤ Today, our goal is to check ATTITUDES....

PROPS:
Take some casual pictures of people displaying attitude...without them knowing what you are doing...

---

1 Kings 11:9-11 (NIV)   The LORD became angry with Solomon because his heart had turned away from the LORD, the God of Israel, who had appeared to him twice. [10] Although he had forbidden Solomon to follow other gods, Solomon did not keep the Lord's command. [11] So the LORD said to Solomon, "_Since this is your attitude and you have not kept my covenant and my decrees, which I commanded you, I will most certainly tear the kingdom away from you_ and give it to one of your subordinates.

➢ Because of God's love for Solomon's father, David, God promised not to tear the kingdom away from him, but not in his life time

➢ One might ask…why does it matter than…if he knows it, but wont live to see it?

➢ It is because, the curse will fall upon his offspring.

➢ We can take things upon ourselves much easier than we can seeing or knowing our children will have to go through something.

➢ YOU BETTER WATCH YOUR ATTITUDE!!! BECAUSE GOD IS WATCHING YOU!!!

Ephesians 4:17-24 (NIV)   So I tell you this, and insist on it in the Lord, that you must no longer live as the Gentiles do, in the futility of their thinking. [18] They are darkened in their understanding and separated from the life of God because of the ignorance that is in them due to the hardening of their hearts. [19]

Having lost all sensitivity, they have given themselves over to sensuality so as to indulge in every kind of impurity, with a continual lust for more. [20] You, however, did not come to know Christ that way. [21] Surely you heard of him and were taught in him in accordance with the truth that is in Jesus. [22] You were taught, with regard to your former way of life, to put off your old self, which is being corrupted by its deceitful desires; [23] _to be made new in the attitude of your minds_; [24] and to put on the new self, created to be like God in true righteousness and holiness.

➢ Today...we want to re-align or adjust ATTITUDES.
➢ In order to re-align our attitude we must change the way of our thinking.
➢ We need to think pleasant thoughts
➢ We need to think positive thoughts
➢ We need to be upbeat and encouraging
➢ We need to know that 'ALL THINGS WORK TOGETHER FOR THE GOOD!'

Philippians 2:4-7 (NIV) Each of you should look not only to your own interests, but also to the interests of others. [5] _Your attitude should be the same as that of Christ Jesus_: [6] Who, being in very nature God, did not consider equality with God something to be grasped, [7] but made himself nothing, taking the very nature of a servant, being made in human likeness.

- In order to have a good attitude, you must think of others first
- Husbands…you need to consider your wives
- Wives…you need to consider your husbands
- It is like Christmas…everyone is nicer at Christmas…
- NEWS FLASH… EVERYDAY IS CHRISTMAS FOR CHRISTIANS!!!

Colossians 3:12-17 (NIV) Therefore, as _God's chosen people_, holy and dearly loved, clothe yourselves with compassion, kindness, humility, gentleness and patience. [13] _Bear with each other and forgive_ whatever grievances you may have against one another. _Forgive as the Lord forgave you_. [14] And _over all these virtues put on love_, which binds them all together in perfect unity. [15] Let the peace of Christ rule in your hearts, since as members of one body _you were called to peace._ And be thankful. [16] Let the word of Christ dwell in you richly as you teach and admonish one another with all wisdom, and as you sing psalms, hymns and spiritual songs with gratitude in your hearts to God. [17] And _whatever you do_, whether in word or deed, _do it all in the name of the Lord Jesus, giving thanks to God_ the Father through him.

- In order to rid yourself of attitudes….
- One must learn the lesson of forgiveness
- Once you are able to forgive yourself…
- You can also, forgive others.

The last 4 weeks, I have attempted to preach messages on things that slip in the back door of church members lives, while we are trying to judge and condemn other sins that we think is bigger!! In Gods sight…sin is sin.

The fact is:
- ➢ Gossip will send us to hell
- ➢ Stubbornness will send us to hell
- ➢ Our Tempers will send us to hell.
- ➢ And our bad attitudes will send us to hell.

ISN'T IT TIME FOR AN ADJUSTMENT?

52

You CAN DO IT!!!

Props:
Give everyone a piece of conduit about 6 inches long with a label on it U Conduit …. On the platform have a large conduit pipe.

Philippians 4:8-13 (NIV)   Finally, brothers, whatever is true, whatever is noble, whatever is right, whatever is pure, whatever is lovely, whatever is admirable--if anything is excellent or praiseworthy--think about such things. [9] Whatever you have learned or received or heard from me, or seen in me-- put it into practice. And the God of peace will be with you. [10] I rejoice greatly in the Lord that at last you have renewed your concern for me. Indeed, you have been concerned, but you had no opportunity to show it. [11] I am not saying this because I am in need, for I have learned to be content whatever the circumstances. [12] I know what it is to be in need, and I know what it is to have plenty. I have learned the secret of being content in any and every situation, whether well fed or hungry, whether living in plenty or in want. [13]

I can do everything through him who gives me strength.

➢ What do you need in your life today?
➢ Do you truly believe that GOD CAN DO IT?
➢ You need people surrounding you with POSSITIVE reinforcement.
➢ LIKE The Little ENGINE that Could....
➢ I THINK I CAN I THINK I CAN.... (have them to say this...)
➢ Now change it into ...I KNOW I CAN ... I KNOW I CAN...!!!

Job 42:1-2 (NIV) Then Job replied to the LORD: ² "*I know that you can do all things*; no plan of yours can be thwarted.

Matthew 19:26 (NIV) Jesus looked at them and said, "With man this is impossible, but *with God all things are possible*."

➢ Jesus can do ANYTHING!!!
➢ It is us that puts boundaries and limits on him....
➢ We should never put Jesus is a box....

Mark 9:23 (NIV) ..."*Everything is possible* for him who believes."

➢ What miracle do you need in your life today...
➢ You need to remember...

310

➢ U CONDUIT… (YOU CAN DO IT)
➢ LET this prop… be a center piece for questions…and them remind people that they can do all things through Christ.

Romans 8:35-39 (NIV) Who shall separate us from the love of Christ? Shall trouble or hardship or persecution or famine or nakedness or danger or sword? [36] As it is written: "For your sake we face death all day long; we are considered as sheep to be slaughtered." [37] No, in all these things we are more than conquerors through him who loved us. [38] _For I am convinced_ that neither death nor life, neither angels nor demons, neither the present nor the future, nor any powers, [39] neither height nor depth, nor anything else in all creation, will _be able to separate us from the love of God that is in Christ Jesus our Lord_.

➢ David….
➢ Though he was young and inexperienced…
➢ When he saw Goliath he said… I CAN DO IT!!!
➢ When Caleb went into the Valley of Eshcol
➢ No matter the size of the enemy, he declared…WE CAN DO IT
➢ When Shadrach, Meshach, and Abednego faced the fiery furnace…
➢ They didn't bow down…they looked into the furnace and declared…WE CAN DO IT!!!
➢ When Daniel faced the lions in the den…

➤ He looked out and proclaimed....I CAN DO IT!!!!

2 Chronicles 20:15-17 (NIV) He said: "Listen, King Jehoshaphat and all who live in Judah and Jerusalem! This is what the LORD says to you: _'Do not be afraid or discouraged because of this vast army_.(SOMEONE SHOUT... I CAN DO IT!!!!) For the battle is not yours, but God's. ¹⁶ Tomorrow march down against them. They will be climbing up by the Pass of Ziz, and you will find them at the end of the gorge in the Desert of Jeruel. ¹⁷ _You will not have to fight this battle. Take up your positions; stand firm and see the deliverance the LORD will give you_, (SHOUT... I CAN DO IT) O Judah and Jerusalem. Do not be afraid; do not be discouraged. Go out to face them tomorrow, and the LORD will be with you.'" (SHOUT ... I CAN DO IT)

Proverbs 23:7 (KJV) For as a man thinketh in his heart, so is he.....

53

You can't SINK my Battleship

Satan knows that you are cruising forward in you life:

➤ You have successfully grown up and began to make something out of your life… even when the odds were against you.
➤ You made it through college even though it was tough
➤ You mended your marriage or survived your divorce
➤ You got your children through school
➤ You received your promotion

SATAN KNOWS YOUR CRUISING FROWARD IN YOUR LIFE!!!

THEREFORE…HE WANTS TO SINK YOUR BATTLESHIP!!!

Satan is under water looking through his periscope trying to see who is a float…

- He sees you cruising toward your greatest blessing....
- He will try to send torpedo's through the water to sink your hopes and dreams...
- He wants to kill your promises that God has birthed in you!!!

1 Peter 5:6-11 (NIV)   Humble yourselves, therefore, under God's mighty hand, that he may lift you up in due time. [7] Cast all your anxiety on him because he cares for you. [8] Be self-controlled and alert. *Your enemy the devil prowls around like a roaring lion looking for someone to devour.* [9] Resist him, standing firm in the faith, because you know that your brothers throughout the world are undergoing the same kind of sufferings. [10] And the God of all grace, who called you to his eternal glory in Christ, after you have suffered a little while, will himself restore you and make you strong, firm and steadfast. [11] To him be the power for ever and ever. Amen.

BUT REMEMBER THIS: OUR WEAPONS ARE GREATER

SATAN CANT SINK YOUR BATTLESHIP

Ephesians 6:11-13 (NIV)   Put on the full armor of God so that you can take your stand against the devil's schemes. [12] For our

struggle is not against flesh and blood, but against the rulers, against the authorities, against the powers of this dark world and against the spiritual forces of evil in the heavenly realms. [13] Therefore put on the full armor of God, so that when the day of evil comes, you may be able to stand your ground, and after you have done everything, to stand.

OUR COMMANDER IS VICTORIOUS

Jude 1:21-25 (NIV) Keep yourselves in God's love as you wait for the mercy of our Lord Jesus Christ to bring you to eternal life. [22] Be merciful to those who doubt; [23] snatch others from the fire and save them; to others show mercy, mixed with fear--hating even the clothing stained by corrupted flesh. [24] To him who is able to keep you from falling and to present you before his glorious presence without fault and with great joy-- [25] to the only God our Savior be glory, majesty, power and authority, through Jesus Christ our Lord, before all ages, now and forevermore! Amen.

Psalms 47:7-8 (NIV) For God is the King of all the earth; sing to him a psalm of praise. [8] God reigns over the nations; God is seated on his holy throne.

REMEMBER....

➢ When you are under attack

➤ Even Hell knows you are getting ready to receive your greatest blessing.

SATAN CANT SINK YOUR BATTLESHIP!!!

WHERE SIN (SATAN) ABOUNDS...GRACE (GOD) MUCH MORE ABOUNDS.

Romans 5:20 (KJV) Moreover the law entered, that the offence might abound. But where sin abounded, grace did much more abound:

Romans 5:20 (NIV) The law was added so that the trespass might increase. But where sin increased, grace increased all the more,

➤ When Satan attacks your finances....guess what... your finances are about to be blessed
➤ When Satan attacks your children...guess what...your children are about to be blessed
➤ When Satan attacks your marriage...guess what...your marriage is about to be blessed
➤ When Satan attacks your mind...guess what...your mind is about to be blessed
➤ When Satan attacks your body... guess what...your body is about to be blessed

SATAN CANT SINK YOUR BATTLESHIP

- Ignore the ones cursing and throwing stones at you!!! Keep your focus.
- When we stay focused on Jesus, Satan will drop his stones and walk away
- If we don't acknowledge him or his cursings.

Deuteronomy 28:1-13 (NIV) If you fully obey the LORD your God and carefully follow all his commands I give you today, the LORD your God will set you high above all the nations on earth. [2] All these blessings will come upon you and accompany you if you obey the LORD your God: [3] You will be blessed in the city and blessed in the country. [4] The fruit of your womb will be blessed, and the crops of your land and the young of your livestock--the calves of your herds and the lambs of your flocks. [5] Your basket and your kneading trough will be blessed. [6] You will be blessed when you come in and blessed when you go out. [7] _The LORD will grant that the enemies who rise up against you will be defeated before you. They will come at you from one direction but flee from you in seven._ [8] The LORD will send a blessing on your barns and on everything you put your hand to. The LORD your God will bless you in the land he is giving you. [9] The LORD will establish you as his holy people, as he promised you on oath, if you keep the commands of the LORD your God and walk in his ways. [10] Then all the peoples on earth will see that you are called by the name of the LORD, and they will fear you. [11]

The LORD will grant you abundant prosperity--in the fruit of your womb, the young of your livestock and the crops of your ground--in the land he swore to your forefathers to give you. [12] **The LORD will open the heavens, the storehouse of his bounty, to send rain on your land in season and to bless all the work of your hands. You will lend to many nations but will borrow from none.** [13] **The LORD will make you the head, not the tail. If you pay attention to the commands of the LORD your God that I give you this day and carefully follow them, you will always be** at the top, never at the bottom.

Satan....cant sink my BATTLESHIP!!!THE BATTLE IS ON!!!!

54

You Got issues???

There was a woman in the Bible, that we often read about...that had a serious problem. She had some a MAJOR "issue" going on in her life.

How many of you know someone ... who always has some drama in there life?
- ➤ Always.... DRAMA DRAMA DRAMA
- ➤ There is some folks that just have to have ISSUES in their lives.

- ➤ You may have an issue with your X
- ➤ You may have issues with your spouse
- ➤ You may have issues with your boyfriend
- ➤ You may have issues with your dog...
- ➤ People today are just filled up with ISSUES...

This woman in the Bible...
Her issue was bleeding.... What is your issue?

Look at your neighbor and tell them... "YOU GOT ISSUE"

Mark 5:21-27 (KJV) ... when Jesus was passed over again by ship unto the other side, much people gathered unto him: and he was nigh unto the sea. [22] And, behold, there cometh one of the rulers of the synagogue, Jairus by name; and when he saw him, he fell at his feet, [23] And besought him greatly, saying, My little daughter lieth at the point of death: I pray thee, come and lay thy hands on her, that she may be healed; and she shall live. [24] And Jesus went with him; and much people followed him, and thronged him. [25] _And a certain woman, which had an issue of blood twelve years, [26] And had suffered many things of many physicians, and had spent all that she had, and was nothing bettered, but rather grew worse, [27] When she had heard of Jesus, came in the press behind, and touched his garment._

YOU NEED TO PRESS YOUR WAY THROUGH AND TOUCH JESUS ABOUT YOUR ISSUES!!!!

- ➤ Jesus had just finished teaching the disciples about fasting
- ➤ When all the sudden He was interrupted by a ruler
- ➤ Begging for Jesus to come and touch his dieing daughter so she could live
- ➤ Jesus gets up to go take care of this situation when…
- ➤ A woman with an issue came up and touched Him!!!

Mark 5:28-34 (KJV) For she said, _If I may touch but his clothes, I shall be whole_. [29] And straightway *the fountain of her blood (ISSUE) was dried up*; and she felt in her body that she was healed of *(HER ISSUE)* that plague. [30] And Jesus, immediately knowing in himself that virtue had gone out of him, turned him about in the press, and said, Who touched my clothes? [31] And his disciples said unto him, Thou seest the multitude thronging thee, and sayest thou, Who touched me? [32] And he looked round about to see her that had done this thing. [33] But the woman fearing and trembling, knowing what was done in her, came and fell down before him, and told him all the truth. [34] And he said unto her, Daughter, thy faith hath made thee whole; go in peace, and be whole of thy *(ISSUE IN WHICH YOU CAME WITH)* plague.

➤ You better be careful of who you allow to touch you!!!
➤ There are some folks with some issues ....
➤ That you don't need to let them lay hands on you!!!
➤ Don't let just anyone lay hands on you!!!
➤ This woman however... was wanting a touch by the MASTER...
➤ We need to make sure that we know where our virtue flows from.

THIS WOMAN IN THE BIBLE WITH HER ISSUE...WAS WILLING TO GO WHERE EVER

SHE HAD TO GO AND DO WHATEVER IT
TOOK TO RID HERSELF OF IT!!!

> Do you want deliverance bad enough to touch Jesus in a way that will make virtue flow from Him into you?

- ➤ You have got to want it!!!
- ➤ You have got to be willing to pay the price…
- ➤ You may have to change some things
- ➤ You may have to redo some things
- ➤ BUT the virtue can flow from HIM into you …

- ➤ Zacheus had an issue of STEALING…WHAT IS YOUR ISSUE?
- ➤ Ananias and Saphirra had the issue of LIEING…WHAT IS YOUR ISSUE?
- ➤ Jacob had an Issue of JEALOUSY…WHAT IS YOUR ISSUE?
- ➤ Rich Young Ruler had the Issue of his love for MONEY…WHAT IS YOUR ISSUE?

CAN I TELL YOU WHAT YOUR ISSUE IS…
????

YOUR ISSUE… IS U

- ➤ The truth of the mater is…
- ➤ Our X is not our issue… our un forgiveness is…
- ➤ Our Spouse is not our issue…We have issues ourselves
- ➤ Our ISSUE…really does lie within US…
- ➤ YOUR ISSUE …. IS U

NOW… HOW DO WE DEAL WITH IT…

- ➤ We press our way through to Jesus…
- ➤ We touch the hem of his garment…
- ➤ We leave our Issues with Him…
- ➤ We live a HAPPY life…

WHAT ARE YOUR ISSUES????

AREN'T YOU TIRED OF CARRYING THEM AROUND.

Psalms 55:22 (KJV) Cast thy burden upon the LORD, and he shall sustain thee: he shall never suffer the righteous to be moved.

55

You gotta Eat!!!!

Props-
A table set for dinner, checkers food. You need about $50 in Checkers gift certificates...You need the theme throughout the church and the song..."YOU GOTTA EAT".

Matthew 5:6 Blessed *are* they who hunger and thirst after righteousness! For they shall be filled. (MKJV)

When Jesus talked to people He met them where they were. It is evident that we as a people love to eat. Jesus, no doubt, loved to eat, seeing how He used hunger and thirsting to show ones desire for food.

Points about being hungry

      a. It effects people differently

➤ Some may get a headache

➤ Others get light headed

➤ Some people get real irritable.

Why? Because you need to eat.

Spiritually, you are worried, when you gotta eat...
having:

> ➢ Mood swings
> ➢ Snapping on folk
> ➢ Or simply not able to function.

Guess what, "You gotta eat." Pick up God's word and feast on it.

> ➢ Some times you are hungry but don't know what you have a taste for.
> ➢ So you snack on one thing, but you are not satisfied.
> ➢ You try something else, and you are still not satisfied.
> ➢ Next thing you know, you have eaten so much, you are now sick, and not satisfied.

Spiritually

> ➢ You go to this revival, still not satisfied,
> ➢ you go to this conference, not satisfied.
> ➢ You go from place to place looking for something and all you need to do is sit at the table and eat what is set before you.

Psalms 34:8 (KJV) O taste and see that the LORD is good: blessed is the man[that trusteth in him.

a. Sometimes you are so hungry that you eat too fast. (Let one of the people act like they are eating fast.)

> ➤ Eating too fast can make you overeat and thus making you sick.
> ➤ Spiritually, we don't have time to sit down and eat, so we say a quick, half hearted prayer, read a verse or two and wonder why we don't have any power.
> ➤ Why the Devil is whipping up on us and we are failing test and falling left and right. You ATE TOO FAST!!!

It's not the quantity, but quality. If you only have a few minutes take your time and give God all of those few minutes.

d. Then we have the hungry/picky eater.

> ➤ You are hungry but you want to eat only what you want, more than likely junk food.
> ➤ Instead of eating at the table, you grab some chips, a candy bar and end up **malnourished**.
> ➤ Picking and choosing what you want to eat.
> ➤ Spiritually, you choose what you want to eat, you'll enjoy the word about blessings, but you don't want to tithe.

➤ You'll enjoy the word on healing but won't let go of your STRONGHOLD, whatever it is, lying, cheating, backbiting, fornicating, and etc.

e.   Then there are those that have a eating disorder.

➤ They have what they call **"Binge and Purge".**
➤ This is where the person eats and eats and once they are done that same person will make themselves throw up not to gain weight.
➤ Spiritually, you will spend hours reading the word, reading spiritual book and then turn around and live a sinful life.
➤ You can quote the Bible back and forward but you throw it up when you choose to sin on purpose.

f.   Those that **Binge and Purge** develop a disease called **Bulimia** - a condition in which bouts of overeating are followed by under -eating, use of laxatives, or self-induced vomiting.

➤ It is associated with depression and anxiety about putting on weight.
➤ And sometimes they will begin to vomit without making themselves, your body will

just automatically do it because it is used to rejecting the food.

> The same is spiritually, once you keep making yourself not receive the word, you will automatically reject the word, "Oh, that ain't for me." Or "So and so needed to hear that…" Or just hear the word and do what you want to do.

Fat Vs.Slim

One thing about being overweight is people don't think you need to eat. People who are overweight could get comments like, "You don't need to eat…" or "you are already fat, you don't need nothing to eat." But if you are hungry, guess what, "**_You gotta eat_**." Spiritually, you will see someone anointed, fat in the spirit, and think they got it they don't need to read as often as the next, but no matter how fat you are in the spirit, if you are hungry, you have to eat.

Luke 12:48 But he that knew not, and did commit things worthy of stripes, shall be beaten with few stripes. For unto whomsoever much is given, of him shall be much required: and to whom men have committed much, of him they will ask the more.

One thing Dr. Hill taught us in the last session was not to eat and drink and the same time. The Bible has the "rule of first mention" it says hunger and then thirst. Dr. Hill says "eat first, then drink." If you don't the liquid between the eating disturbs the acids that are to break down your food, thus causing heart burn and indigestion.

> ➢ Spiritually, you eat the word but water it down to make it say what you want to say and you end up with spiritual heart burn.
> ➢ Wrong decisions, wrong attitudes, falling into sin because the word was interrupted from breaking down the food right with the water you drank in between.
> ➢ God's word says, love your enemies, yet you hold grudges, indigestion. The word says pay your tithes and offering and you give 1% instead of 10% and you bring a curse on you and your house, you get indigestion.

Let's deal with being filled.
When we are full the main thing a lot of people want to do is go to sleep.

> ➢ That is what God wants us to do, fill up on His word and rest in Him.
> ➢ Knowing that when we stand still (rest. Sleep), in Him, he will fight our battles.
> ➢ The battle is the Lord's.
> ➢ So when we are full of the word, we know that we can rightfully rest.

➤ So instead of dieting, or skipping meals, if you are hungry remember, *"You Gotta Eat"*.

56

YOU GOTTA GET PREPARED!!!

> **PROPS:**
> YOU NEED A GIANT "PREPARATION H" BOX MADE TO LOOK LIKE THE REAL THING...ABOUT 2 OR 3 FEET LONG. YOU WILL ALSO NEED SEVERAL SMALL BOXES OF "PREPARATION H" TO HAVE LAYING AROUND THE ALTAR. (DO NOT PUT THEM IN VIEWING DISTANCE...YOU WILL BRING THEM OUT...MID SERMON)

1 Corinthians 1:26-31 (NIV) Brothers, think of what you were when you were called. *Not many of you were wise by human standards; not many were influential; not many were of noble birth.* [27] *But God chose the foolish things of the world to shame the wise; God chose the weak things of the world to shame the strong.* [28] *He chose the lowly things of this world and the despised things--and the things that are not--to nullify the things that are,* [29] so that no one may boast before him.

³⁰ It is because of him that you are in Christ Jesus, who has become for us wisdom from God--that is, our righteousness, holiness and redemption. ³¹ Therefore, as it is written: "Let him who boasts boast in the Lord."

My mind is always…looking for a new sermon idea…relating us back to some familiar thing that all of us see in our every day lives…. And when I looked up…there it was … right in front of me….PREPARATION H!!!

We are all familiar with this product…PREPARATION H… It can be used for more than one thing….

> ➢ I think that all of us are aware of the purpose it was made for…
> ➢ But did you know… that it has been proven….

That a little dab under the eyes will iron out any bags or wrinkles????

NOW GOD SURELY CAN'T MINISTER TO US…THROUGH A PRODUCT LIKE THIS…. OR CAN HE….

I realized that for all of my life… I have been in PREPARATION:

> ➢ In Grade school in my younger years I learned to read

- In high school, in my teen years, I learned to get over my nervousness in front of crowd in FFA
- In college, in my twenties... I learned about the Bible...and the stories that lied in its covers
- In my masters degree in my 30's I learned how to lead,
- In my doctorate program in my 40's, I am still in PREPARATION, to become what God has for me...
- MY LIFE HAS BEEN FILLED WITH PREPARATION!!!
- Now I must PREPARE to get my BLESSING
- Now I must PREPARE to get my VICTORY
- Now I must PREPARE to get my ABUNANCE
- Now I must PREPARE to get my HEALING
- Now I must PREPARE to get my DELIVERANCE

WE SPEND A LOT OF TIME IN OUR LIFE PREPARING:
- Preparing for a wedding
- Preparing for our food
- Preparing for school
- Preparing for work

THE TRUTH IS...WE SPEND A LOT OF TIME
PREPARING FOR THINGS...

LET ME TELLYOU WHAT I SAW WHEN I
SAW:

PREPARATION H

I SAW :

PREPARATION H-EAVEN !!!

What is our purpose on Earth... ????
> ➢ To prepare for heaven
> ➢ This is just practice...
> ➢ I heard Bishop Freeman say... I hope you
>   like things loud...
> ➢ Because in heaven ... everyone is going to
>   be shouting
> ➢ And in Hell...everyone is going to be
>   screaming...
> ➢ Our praise here on earth...is only a
>   practice of what we will do for thousands
>   of years in heaven.

EVEN GOD PREPARES:

**John 14:1-4 (NIV) "Do not let your hearts be
troubled. Trust in God ; trust also in me. [2] In**

my Father's house are many rooms; if it were not so, I would have told you. _I am going there to prepare a place for you_. ³ And _if I go and prepare a place for you, I will come back and take you to be with me_ that you also may be where I am. ⁴ You know the way to the place where I am going."

The Bible speaks of preparing…nearly 100 times…
  ➤ Get prepared
  ➤ Prepare the way
  ➤ Make Preparation
  ➤ Be prepared…. Etc.

MY "PREPARAION H" STANDS FOR PREPARATION HEAVEN!!!
I AM PREPARING TO GO TO A PLACE…WHERE THEY KNOW HOW TO PRAISE:

Revelation 19:1 (NIV) After this I heard what sounded like the roar of a _great multitude in heaven shouting:_ "Hallelujah! Salvation and glory and power belong to our God,

Revelation 19:4-7 (NIV) The twenty-four elders and the four living _creatures fell down and worshiped God_, who was seated on the throne. And _they cried: "Amen, Hallelujah!"_ ⁵ _Then a voice came from the throne, saying: "Praise our God_, all you his servants, you who fear him, both small and great!" ⁶ Then _I heard what sounded like a great multitude, like the roar of rushing waters and like loud_

peals of thunder, shouting: "Hallelujah! For our Lord God Almighty reigns. [7] Let us rejoice and be glad and give him glory! For the wedding of the Lamb has come, and his bride has made herself ready.

Revelation 21:3-7 (NIV) And *I heard a loud voice from the throne saying, "Now the dwelling of God is with men, and he will live with them. They will be his people, and God himself will be with them and be their God.* [4] *He will wipe every tear from their eyes. There will be no more death or mourning or crying or pain, for the old order of things has passed away."* [5] He who was seated on the throne said, "I am making everything new!" Then he said, "Write this down, for these words are trustworthy and true." [6] He said to me: "It is done. I am the Alpha and the Omega, the Beginning and the End. To him who is thirsty I will give to drink without cost from the spring of the water of life. [7] He who overcomes will inherit all this, and I will be his God and he will be my son.

Revelation 1:7-8 (NIV) Look, *he is coming with the clouds*, and every eye will see him, even those who pierced him; and all the peoples of the earth will mourn because of him. So shall it be! Amen. [8] "I am the Alpha and the Omega," says the Lord God, "who is, and who was, and who is to come, the Almighty."

PREPARE TO MEET HIM

PREPARE TO REIGN WITH HIM
PREPARE TO BE WITH HIM FOR AN ETERNITY
PREPARE TO PRAISE HIM
PREPARE TO WORSHIP HIM
PREPARE…PREPARE…PREPARE!!!!!

Illustrated Sermons
for use by ministers to
aid in preparation of
sermons
$10.00

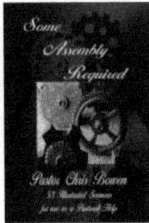

The personal
testimony of the life
and ministry of
Pastor Chris Bowen
$10.00

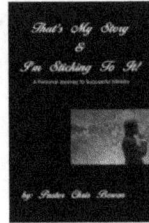

A study guiding the
reader through the
book of Job one
chapter at a time
$10.00

A study guiding the
reader through the
book of Romans one
chapter at a time
$10.00

An indepth study of
the book of
Revelation providing
insight of what is to
come
$10.00

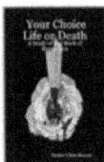

A source of wisdom
on how to live a debt
free life as God has
ordained
$17.00

Most recent work:

In this personal testimony,
Pastor Chris Bowen openly
shares his experience of how his
own trust in God was tested.

Two Nights
With The
Devil

By: Pastor Chris Bowen

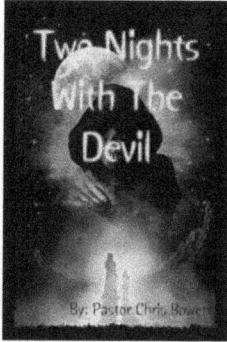

Swung Open or Swollen Shut - $17.00
All other publications - $10.00

To order copies of these publications:

Visit our website: www.livingfaithtabernacle.com

Or Contact the Church:

Living Faith Tabernacle
5880 Old Dixie Road
Forest Park, GA 30297

(404) 361-0812

You may also contact Dr. Christopher Bowen direct at:
pastorchrislft@aol.com

www.ingramcontent.com/pod-product-compliance
Lightning Source LLC
LaVergne TN
LVHW011216080426
835509LV00005B/162